Joint Interagency Task Force–South: The Best Known, Least Understood Interagency Success

Joint Interagency Task Force–South: The Best Known, Least Understood Interagency Success

By Evan Munsing and Christopher J. Lamb

Institute for National Strategic Studies
Strategic Perspectives, No. 5

Series Editor: Phillip C. Saunders

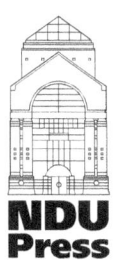

National Defense University Press
Washington, D.C.
June 2011

First printing, June 2011

For current publications of the Institute for National Strategic Studies, please go to the National Defense University Web site at: www.ndu.edu/inss.

Contents

Executive Summary 1

Introduction 3

Interagency Coordination and Cross-functional Teams 4

Drugs as a National Security Problem 6

Legislative Solutions. 10

JIATF–South's Predecessor: Joint Task Force–4. 12

Austerity Spurs Innovation: NICCP 1993 and 1994 16

Early Years of the JIATFs: 1994 to 1998 19

JIATF–East Lays the Foundation for JIATF–South: 1999 to 2003. 22

JIATF–South: The "Gold Standard" for Interagency Operations. 30

Performance Variables. 30

Maintaining Effectiveness: 2004 to Present 69

Observations. 76

Conclusion 82

Notes 87

About the Authors 105

This research is dedicated to the pioneering men and women of JIATF–South, who have shown the Nation a better way.

Executive Summary

Joint Interagency Task Force–South (JIATF–South) is well known within the U.S. Government as the "gold standard" for interagency cooperation and intelligence fusion, despite its preference for keeping a low profile and giving other agencies the credit for its successes. It is often cited as a model for whole-of-government problem-solving in the literature on interagency collaboration, and other national security organizations have tried to copy its approach and successes. Despite the plaudits and attention, the way that JIATF–South actually operates has only received superficial analysis. In fact, few people actually understand why JIATF–South works as well as it does or how its success might be replicated.

This study attempts to fill the gap in knowledge about JIATF–South as a model for cross-organizational collaboration. It traces the evolution of the task force from its roots in the "War on Drugs" in the 1980s, through its original manifestation as Joint Task Force–4 in the early 1990s and its later reinvention as Joint Interagency Task Force–East (and still later, its renaming as JIATF–South), up until the present day. It then examines how JIATF–South actually works with the help of 10 organizational performance variables taken from organizational and management research on cross-functional teams. Investigating JIATF–South's performance through these different organizational lenses, and weighing the importance of each variable in light of JIATF–South's historical experience, yields a compelling explanation for JIATF–South's stellar performance. The results contribute to a better understanding of interagency teams and help answer the pressing question of whether successes like JIATF–South can be replicated elsewhere in the national security system.

Introduction

In 2009, a single U.S. Government organization accounted for more than 40 percent of global cocaine interdiction.[1] It coordinated the disruption of approximately 220 tons of cocaine, with disruption defined as the unrecoverable loss of the drugs through direct seizure, forced jettisoning by the trafficker, or other courses of action.[2] During the same time, the rest of the U.S. Government seized only 40 tons.[3] Over the past 20 years, the same organization has arrested some 4,600 traffickers, captured nearly 1,100 vessels, and deprived drug cartels of $190 billion in profits.[4] Although the importance of drug interdiction as opposed to other counterdrug programs and activities may be debated, it is clear that this organization—JIATF–South—is a matchless operational success. Within the U.S. Government it has earned a reputation as the "gold standard"[5] and "crown jewel"[6] of interagency cooperation and intelligence fusion. Each year thousands of people visit JIATF–South[7] to see how it seamlessly coordinates the efforts of local, Federal, and international forces in the war on drugs:

> *A typical case can start with JIATF–South receiving actionable law enforcement information from the DEA* [Drug Enforcement Administration]. *This prompts the deployment of a* [Customs and Border Protection (CBP)] *P–3 or Coast Guard C–130 that subsequently detects and monitors a foreign flagged suspect vessel until JIATF–South can sortie a Coast Guard cutter or U.S. Navy or allied surface ship with an embarked Law Enforcement Detachment (LEDET) to intercept. When the ship arrives on scene* [there is] *a shift of tactical control from JIATF–South to the* [Coast Guard]. *For a foreign flag vessel, the Coast Guard tactical commander implements a bilateral agreement or arrangement in force with the vessel's flag state to confirm registry and to stop, board and search the vessel for drugs. If drugs are found, jurisdiction and disposition over the vessel, drugs and crew are coordinated with the State Department, DOJ* [Department of Justice], *and the flag state.*[8]

Although JIATF–South tries to keep a low profile, its success (and location in Key West, Florida) makes it the destination of choice for anyone interested in forging interagency coordination in the field. The 7,000 to 10,000 visitors hosted by JIATF–South each year typically stay briefly and depart without really understanding how or why the Task Force works so successfully. JIATF–South is also treated superficially in most of the literature on interagency collaboration, frequently identified as a model for whole-of-government problem-solving but with little attention paid to how it actually works.[9]

This case study of JIATF–South offers an in-depth explanation for its stellar performance. The purpose is not to evaluate the success or failure of the war on drugs, or to examine current counterdrug policies and their merits.[10] Rather, it is to examine in depth how one remarkably successful interagency counterdrug organization functions and to help answer the pressing question of whether its interagency successes can be replicated elsewhere in the national security system. Many commentators are aware that JIATF–South's success is unusual for an interagency effort but conclude it is a one-of-a-kind organization that cannot be replicated quickly or perhaps at all. The research results offered here dispute that popular conclusion.

We first offer a brief explanation for why interagency collaboration is increasingly important to national security, followed by a historical review of JIATF–South's precursor organizations and explanations of why they proved inadequate. Then, using 10 organizational performance variables extracted from the literature on cross-functional teams, we explain JIATF–South's performance in detail. We close by extracting as many insights as possible from the JIATF–South experience. We explain why we believe JIATF–South's success can be duplicated, and why interagency cross-functional teams in general merit more attention from national security leaders.

Interagency Coordination and Cross-functional Teams

Today's national security challenges "lend themselves to increasingly 'whole of government'" solutions that "will require structural and cultural changes in the executive and legislative branches."[11] Better interagency (or whole-of-government) organizational constructs are a common recommendation in national security reports and commentary,[12] but the practical knowledge to act with confidence on these proposals is far less evident. There is a vast amount of organizational literature on teams[13] and some historical experience with interagency teams in the national security system. However, research on interagency teams per se is rare, and there is little effort by the national security system to codify lessons learned from interagency team experience. This remains true even though it is widely acknowledged that interagency collaboration within the U.S. Government needs to improve and that interagency teams are a promising means toward that end. Interagency teams are cross-functional teams. JIATF–South, as the commander of U.S. Southern Command (USSOUTHCOM) recently noted, is a cross-functional team in every respect:

> *This group, beyond doubt, is a team: a joint, interagency, international, combined and allied team—a creative and innovative body that defines "synergy," the blending*

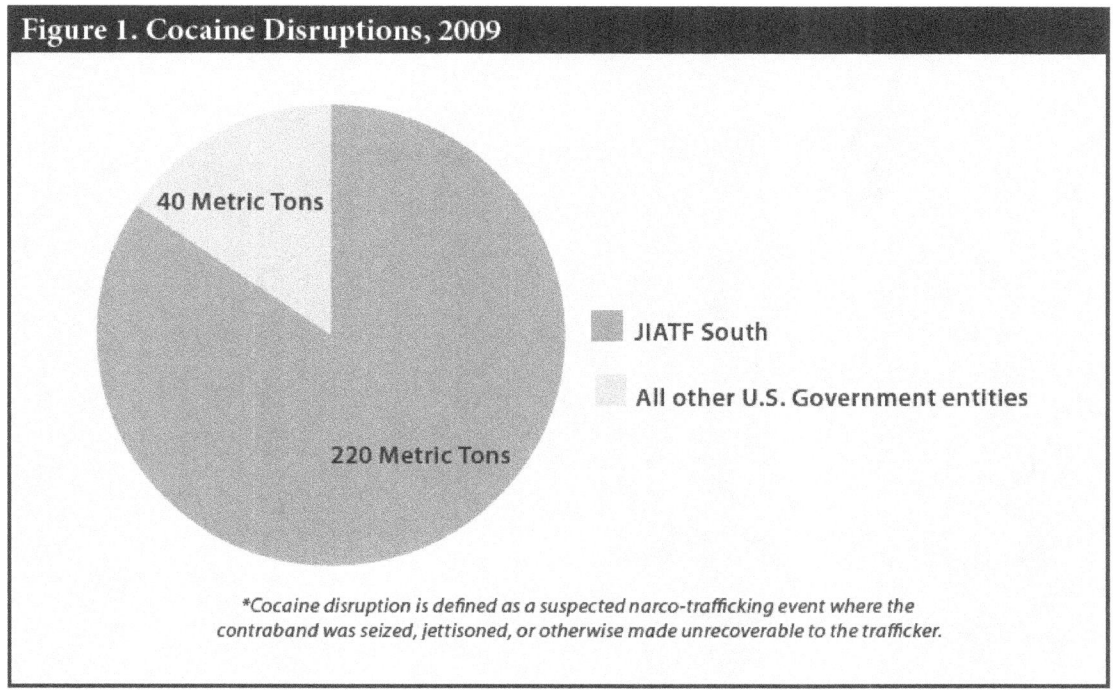

Figure 1. Cocaine Disruptions, 2009

40 Metric Tons

JIATF South

All other U.S. Government entities

220 Metric Tons

Cocaine disruption is defined as a suspected narco-trafficking event where the contraband was seized, jettisoned, or otherwise made unrecoverable to the trafficker.

of experience, professionalism and knowledge being greater than the sum of its individual parts. This kind of success demands total commitment from the entire organization—inspirational leadership, complete integration, collaboration and partnership which exists at every level throughout the command. JIATF–South is the standard for integrating and synchronizing "whole of government," "whole of nation," and "whole of many nations" solutions in confronting challenges to our national and shared regional security.[14]

The 4 branches of the military, 9 different agencies, and 11 partner nations[15] contributing to JIATF–South perform many different functions, but do so as a team. Examining JIATF–South as a cross-functional team allows us to better understand how it operates and thus how it might be replicated, thereby meeting an increasingly urgent requirement for the national security system.

JIATF–South, a widely acknowledged cross-functional, interagency team success, is thus a good place to begin more serious study of interagency teams and organizations. To adequately explain JIATF–South's performance, it is necessary to consider the full range of organizational performance variables for a cross-functional team. Before doing so, however, it is first necessary

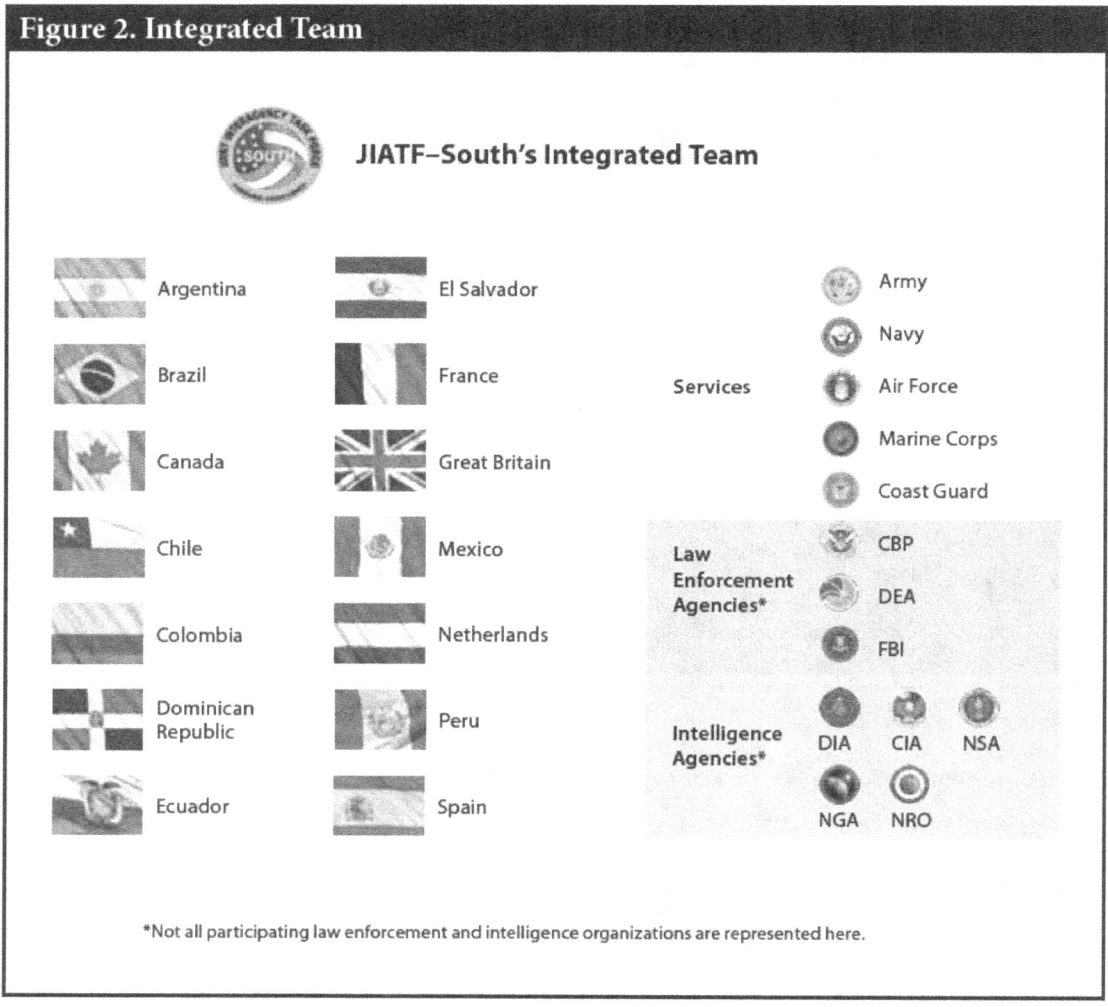

Figure 2. Integrated Team

JIATF–South's Integrated Team

Argentina

Brazil

Canada

Chile

Colombia

Dominican Republic

Ecuador

El Salvador

France

Great Britain

Mexico

Netherlands

Peru

Spain

Services

Army

Navy

Air Force

Marine Corps

Coast Guard

Law Enforcement Agencies*

CBP

DEA

FBI

Intelligence Agencies*

DIA   CIA   NSA

NGA   NRO

*Not all participating law enforcement and intelligence organizations are represented here.

to explain how the organization, its mission, and methods have evolved over time. JIATF–South and its predecessor organizations suffered numerous failures before a winning organizational combination came together. In this regard, JIATF–South constitutes a national experiment of sorts. Understanding each phase of the experiment illuminates the importance of the diverse organizational elements ultimately put in place.

Drugs as a National Security Problem

The JIATF–South story properly begins in the 1980s with the rise of powerful Colombian drug cartels that brought a wave of cocaine and crime to the United States. The Reagan administration and Congress struggled through a path of trial and error in trying to apply traditional

USCG (Eric Willis)

After an 8-day search effort the Customs and Border Protection, U.S. Coast Guard, and Puerto Rico Police Department discover a hidden compartment housing more than a ton of cocaine onboard the motor vessel *Babouth* in February 2004

solutions to the growing threat. Gradually, both the legislative and executive branches realized the drug cartels could not be effectively countered through traditional means and without greater centralized authority for the drug war and the attention of a dedicated, standing national task force. They also came to believe that military support for America's law enforcement agencies engaged in counterdrug operations was necessary.

In 1878, the *Posse Comitatus Act* banned the military from civilian law enforcement activities in order to limit Federal power. A century later, however, the long reach, extensive resources, and great violence of the Colombian cartels were exceeding the ability of civilian law enforcement agencies to contain their activities and threatened to undermine the American law enforcement and legal system. Law enforcement agencies needed access to expensive hardware such as the radar, ships, and airplanes operated by the Department of Defense (DOD). Thus, the *Posse Comitatus Act* was amended in 1981—over the objections of the military Service chiefs—to allow DOD to support civilian law enforcement agencies and the Coast Guard. Although not explicitly stated, congressional intent was clear: the military needed to support law enforcement officers in combating drug smuggling.[16] The amended act continued to bar military personnel from directly participating in law enforcement activities (such as searching or arresting civilians), but it allowed the military to provide technical assistance to law enforcement officers, such as providing transport, intelligence support, and surveillance. In practice this meant that when the military conducted training exercises or redeployed intelligence gathering assets, they would do so in a manner allowing them to support law enforcement activities. For example, law enforcement detachments would be given space on military vessels during training maneuvers. If a suspected drug smuggler was located by the military vessel, the law enforcement agents could board the suspect ship, search it, and arrest its occupants.[17]

The executive branch soon took advantage of the relaxed legal restrictions on DOD participation in the drug war. By 1982, approximately 70 percent of all marijuana and cocaine entering the United States came through southern Florida, valued at $7–12 billion a year.[18] The spike in drug-related violence in Miami, vividly highlighted by the infamous Dadeland Mall Massacre,[19] led to the creation of the first national counterdrug task force, headed by George H.W. Bush. "The Vice President's Task Force on South Florida" combined hundreds of agents from the Drug Enforcement Administration and the Federal Bureau of Investigation (FBI) and drew support from the Customs Service, the Bureau of Alcohol, Tobacco, Firearms, and Explosives, the Internal Revenue Service (IRS), the Army, and the Navy.[20] This Cabinet-level task force targeted traffickers but also went after the bankers and businessmen working with them and offshore banks to launder money. Shutting down South Florida as a drug importation center inadvertently had the effect of rerouting drug shipments to different locations in the United States, forcing the creation of similar "Organized Crime Drug Enforcement Task Forces" in other major cities.[21] Like water following the path of least resistance, drugs found other points of entry along America's porous borders. Frustrated law enforcement officials expressed the need to attack the problem closer to its source by asking whether we should "keep mopping the floor or turn off the faucet."[22]

The following year, the National Narcotics Border Interdiction System was created to coordinate the efforts of all Federal agencies that had either responsibility for preventing drug smuggling or the capability to interdict or prevent drugs from crossing the U.S. border. It would help prioritize targets, make better use of resources, and coordinate interagency operations. Like the Vice President's Task Force, the National Narcotics Border Interdiction System was run by the Vice President and was multidisciplinary, drawing together on its executive board the State Department, Treasury, Defense, Justice, Transportation, Central Intelligence Agency (CIA), the Drug Enforcement Administration, and the White House Drug Abuse

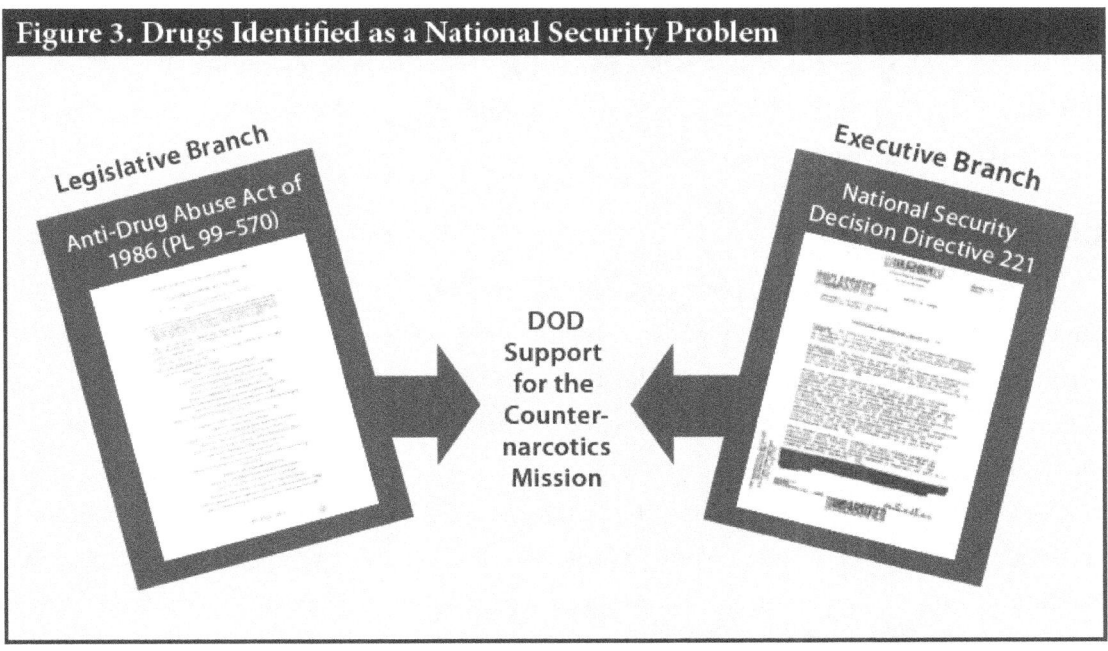

Figure 3. Drugs Identified as a National Security Problem

Legislative Branch

Anti-Drug Abuse Act of 1986 (PL 99–570)

DOD Support for the Counter-narcotics Mission

Executive Branch

National Security Decision Directive 221

Policy Office.[23] Despite its national mission, the National Narcotics Border Interdiction System ended up being primarily focused on monitoring small-airplane traffic from Mexico into the southwestern United States. It eventually dissolved as individual agencies chose to pursue this goal unilaterally.[24]

In 1986, President Reagan took a major step toward institutionalizing DOD support for the war on drugs. National Security Decision Directive 221 declared narcotrafficking a national security threat and authorized the Secretary of Defense to take measures that would "enable U.S. military forces to support counternarcotics efforts more actively."[25] This executive order dovetailed nicely with the *Anti-Drug Abuse Act of 1986* (PL 99–570), which established billets on Navy vessels specifically designated for Coast Guard law enforcement detachments in an effort to increase their ability to intercept drug smugglers.[26] That same year, Customs was told to set up counternarcotic command, control, communications, and intelligence (C³I) centers to enhance interagency coordination on interdiction. The following year, the U.S. Government backed away from the use of interagency task forces under national leadership and instead experimented with using lead agencies to coordinate drug interdiction. Customs became the lead agency for detecting and interdicting trafficking across land borders, and the Coast Guard was the lead for maritime smuggling. They shared responsibilities for air interdiction. Attorney General Edwin Meese extolled the approach, arguing that "Through the lead-agency approach, the American people can look forward to even more effective law enforcement and even greater reduction of drug use." His optimism would prove ill-founded as the lead agency approach did little to improve the coherence of counterdrug efforts or eliminate the "petty jealousies and duplication of effort by law enforcement agencies."[27] Something more radical was needed.

Legislative Solutions

Despite increased resources, greater DOD involvement, and more national attention, the U.S. Government was clearly not winning the drug war. In 1988, with the Medellín cartel firmly in control of the majority of global cocaine distribution, the Senate declared, "The Colombian drug cartels . . . constitute an unprecedented threat, in a nontraditional sense, to the national security of the United States."[28] Congress decided to intervene at multiple levels, beginning with national leadership. The C³I centers Customs had built did not, Congress acknowledged, create an interagency headquarters for the drug war; nor had the National Narcotics Border Interdiction System proven successful. The war on drugs still lacked effective national leadership,[29] and the old idea of centralizing authority for the war on drugs was resurrected. Previous attempts had included the Cabinet-level National Drug Enforcement Policy Board and the White House Office of Drug Abuse Policy, both of which the *Anti-Drug Abuse Act* terminated, as well as the department-level Bureau of Narcotics and Dangerous Drugs under President Lyndon Johnson and the Drug Enforcement Administration under President Richard Nixon.

The *Anti-Drug Abuse Act of 1988* (PL100–690) took another crack at centralization and created the Office of National Drug Control Policy (ONDCP) in the Executive Office of the President. However, rather than acting as an executive agent in its own right, the ONDCP would "provide for coordination among executive branch departments and agencies." This meant that ONDCP was largely restricted to ensuring that the counterdrug strategies of the various departments and agencies of the U.S. Government were in agreement with the President's National Drug Control Strategy.[30] ONDCP could not compel cooperation from anyone and would instead be a coordinating body for the drug war rather than its direct leader.

Congress also reverted to the lead agency approach for some portions of the counterdrug mission. The *National Defense Authorization Act for Fiscal Year* (FY) *1989* designated DOD the lead agency for the detection and monitoring of drug trafficking into the United States, and the Coast Guard as the lead agency for the interdiction and arrest of drug traffickers. This left a significant organizational seam between detection and monitoring on one hand, and interdiction and arrest on the other, but the *National Defense Authorization Act* attempted to paper over the crack by instructing all naval vessels transiting drug interdiction zones or conducting a detection and monitoring mission to carry Coast Guard law enforcement detachments on board.[31]

To implement its new role as lead for detection and monitoring, DOD created several joint task forces with the expectation that they would perform better than Customs' C³I centers. U.S. Pacific Command (USPACOM) created Joint Task Force–5 in Alameda, California, with responsibility for the West Coast; Forces Command created Joint Task Force–6 in El Paso, Texas, with responsibility for the Southwestern border; the North American Aerospace Defense Command (NORAD) created the NORAD Tactical Intelligence Cell at Cheyenne Mountain Air Force Base, Colorado, to monitor airborne trafficking; USSOUTHCOM created a Counterdrug Regional Operations Center for South America; and Atlantic Command created Joint Task Force–4 in Key West, Florida, to monitor the Caribbean. These new organizations were to create C³I nodes that would allow DOD to link its counterdrug efforts with those of civilian law enforcement agencies. Since the United Nations passed the Convention against Illicit Traffic in Narcotic Drugs and Psychotropic Substances in 1988, the United States also had a legal framework for international cooperation on drug enforcement that allowed it to enter into cooperative bilateral arrangements with many of its Caribbean neighbors to interdict and disrupt maritime narcotrafficking.[32]

Thus, by the end of the 1980s, a decade of experimentation had led to several key developments that changed the U.S. approach to counternarcotics. The growing conviction that drugs were a national security matter spurred cooperation between the executive and legislative branches and paved the way for greater involvement by DOD in the war on drugs. A variety of organizational constructs were proposed and used during this period to improve interdiction and support domestic law enforcement agencies. Several innovations—increasing military support for law enforcement agencies, centralizing authority for the war on drugs, and using a lead agency to coordinate U.S. Government efforts—helped but revealed serious shortcomings in how the government was organized for counterdrug missions. It was clear that these innovations could not separately turn the tide on the cartels; to be effective, they would have to be bundled together. This led Congress to designate DOD as lead agency for nondomestic detection and monitoring of suspected drug trafficking events and, in turn, to the creation of the joint task forces (JTFs). Intended to act as a force multiplier for civilian law enforcement agencies, the JTFs centralized efforts for detection and monitoring and combined the lead agency and national task force approach by giving DOD the lead for detection and monitoring but encouraging it to work with interagency partners. The development of task forces for detecting and monitoring the movement of illegal drugs was an important innovation, but it would ultimately prove to be merely a stepping stone in the evolution towards JIATF–South.

JIATF–South's Predecessor: Joint Task Force–4

The Joint Task Force–4 (JTF–4) mission was threefold: to create an intelligence fusion center with a communications network that would allow it to collect and disseminate information; to conduct detection and monitoring missions with DOD assets; and to coordinate interagency detection and monitoring missions.[33] JTF–4, like the other JTFs, was initially dominated by military personnel and run as a military command. Civilians did not have key leadership roles, but there was a small interagency presence. The first commander of JTF–4 was Coast Guard Vice Admiral James Irwin, who was brought out of retirement to command JTF–4 for its first two years because no Service was willing to give up a flag officer to take charge of an untested idea. The DEA, U.S. Customs Service, and the Coast Guard sent liaison personnel and assets to JTF–4 within its first year of operation; other agencies were also given the opportunity to have liaison officers at Key West.[34]

JTF–4 and the other JTFs possessed some particular advantages over civilian counterdrug organizations. Even though DOD was never principally concerned with fighting the war on drugs and kept the JTFs on a shoestring budget,[35] these forces enjoyed substantial resources and many unique assets in comparison to civilian law enforcement agencies. Their headquarters were state-of-the-art command centers (referred to as command, control, communications, computers, and intelligence—or C[4]I—centers) capable of handling both military and interagency assets, and they had access to a wide range of multirole aircraft and ships as well. DOD committed much higher levels of ship days and airplane hours to support the military-dominated JTFs between 1989 and 1993 than it would to support fully interagency task forces in later years. Combining both military and law enforcement assets, JTF–4 had a wider range of hardware to choose from, including surveillance and interdiction aircraft from the Air Force, Navy, Coast Guard, and Customs; patrol boats from the Navy and Coast Guard; intercept boats from Customs; and helicopters from the Army and Customs.

In keeping with the DOD role as lead agency for detection and monitoring beyond U.S. borders, JTFs served primarily as multisource intelligence fusion centers with limited ability to coordinate day-to-day activities of planes and ships performing counterdrug missions. As a military organization, JTF–4 had access to DOD all-source intelligence long coveted by the law enforcement agencies, including national technical means of surveillance. DOD also created an information-sharing network based on its own model to help the exchange of confidential information among the military, intelligence, and law enforcement communities.[36] JTF–4 could gather real-time information from radars owned by the Federal Aviation Administration, NORAD, and the Customs Service and feed this to air and surface assets inside its area of responsibility. It also worked with the El Paso Intelligence Center and the Coast Guard and Customs Joint C³I Center in Miami to collect and analyze intelligence to support their own detection and monitoring operations.[37]

JTF–4 ran into a basic conflict of organizational mandates and cultures when it tried to cultivate law enforcement agencies, especially the DEA, as a source of intelligence about where drugs were coming from and their routes into the United States. Law enforcement culture is sensitive about releasing intelligence and much more patient than the military when pursuing prosecution of suspects. Law enforcement wants to see where drugs go and who is involved in order to arrest and convict as many traffickers as possible. DOD wants to terminate its involvement as soon after detection as possible since it is difficult to continuously track the target and in order to create an appropriate distance from the prosecution of the suspects and stay off of the witness stand.[38] Also, because most of DEA intelligence comes from human sources connected to current investigations, leaked evidence can be dangerous for agents and cases, making DEA liaisons at Key West wary of providing intelligence to JTF–4.[39] The task force was never able to fully earn the trust of DEA liaisons, but in less than a year, it circumvented this problem in part by developing direct relationships with the agency and with State Department Country Teams in Latin America. Where ambassadors proved willing, JTF–4 inserted its own liaisons into the Country Teams. This gave JTF–4 access to a greater range of human intelligence that shed light on smuggling routes and schedules, but sometimes irritated Country Teams wary of military involvement in counterdrug operations.[40] For their part, the DEA and other law enforcement partners were stymied by the propensity of military personnel at JTF–4 to classify intelligence rather than share it with their interagency partners.[41]

Like the other joint task forces, JTF–4 had no dedicated assets for the counterdrug mission; nor could it secure assets in advance. Instead, each day JTF–4 would tell the military Services what it needed to conduct its proposed operations for the next 24 hours and each day the Services would decide what they could spare. Thus, on a daily basis, JTF–4 would have to tailor missions to fit available assets that it did not tactically control. This could be quite difficult, as the equipment available from the different organizations supporting detection and monitoring missions had different strengths and weaknesses in terms of dwell time, range, and other attributes. For example, military aircraft were simply too fast to trail the civilian aircraft used by drug smugglers and thus could not collect the evidence necessary to build a case, and other

USCG (Brian N. Leshak)

Coast Guardsmen watch over 11.5 tons of cocaine seized by the Coast Guard Cutter *Hamilton* from three different vessels in the Eastern Pacific in 2005

aircraft were being deployed without support from surface ships. Detection rates skyrocketed when ships were augmented with helicopters, and both were supported by aircraft.[42] However, it was hard to get civilian and military aircraft that had similar capabilities and endurances,[43] and there were no standard operating procedures for how the military and civilian assets could best work together.[44] Moreover, the Services and civilian agencies were not comfortable operating together. JTF–4 had to tailor each mission to accommodate each Service's preferences on how its assets would be used and under what circumstances. The Coast Guard, DEA, and Customs retained tactical control over the assets they offered JTF–4, and could change or abort missions as they chose. This meant that in practice, aircraft and surface vessels routinely operated under multiple orders from different command centers and pursued different target priorities.

Communications serve as a good example of how difficult operating in this environment could be. The diverse communications systems were not always interoperable, nor did they follow the same security procedures. Some agencies changed their call signs daily for security reasons, which greatly confused those who routinely kept call signs for extended periods of time. At times it was necessary to adopt nonsecure communications systems in order to conduct joint or interagency operations.[45] This was successful but required extra preparation to make sure that everyone followed the same security procedures to minimize the risk of giving away intelligence to the drug traffickers, who were quite good at gathering intelligence on their hunters and in fact occasionally managed to buy some of the JTF–4 operation schedules and plans in advance.[46] Furthermore, although JTF–4 gathered and fused multiple sources of intelligence, its partners did not share a common operating picture. Although there was some information sharing, each agency retained its own intelligence assessments and used them to conduct their own planning and targeting. This impeded the effectiveness of JTF–4's intelligence gathering capabilities, which in any event were too biased toward electronic intelligence. Without human intelligence to cue their assets to look for particular targets, JTF–4 had to sort through many potential targets looking for the one illegitimate shipping or fishing vessel in a sea filled with legitimate traffic. Some detection and monitoring operations were little more than "guys sailing around looking for people."[47]

There were also concerns that the combatant commanders were not adequately supporting and funding the JTFs. The *DOD Appropriations Act, FY 1989* had established a new appropriation, the "Drug Interdiction and Counter-drug Activities," within DOD. In response, the Department created a central transfer account for this new appropriation so funds would be centrally managed and would ensure compliance with congressional intent. The Department also created the role of DOD Coordinator for Drug Enforcement Policy and Support to serve as the Secretary's principal advisor for drug enforcement policy, requirements, priorities, resources, and programs for these responsibilities.[48] The collapse of the Soviet Union also encouraged DOD as a whole to pursue counterdrug operations more vigorously due to fear of budget reductions.[49]

Most important, the experience of the JTFs raised the issue of authority. The commanders of the JTFs only had authority over assigned military personnel, and it became clear early on that the lack of directive authority over interagency plans and operations would lead to confusion and duplication. A 1991 RAND report noted that the JTFs had been overlaid upon or alongside existing military and civilian security and intelligence organizations, many of which had long been involved in drug control. "Little wonder," the report concluded, that it can be "extremely difficult to determine or establish at any one time who is in charge, which organization is supporting and which is supported, and, correspondingly, who reports to whom on what aspect."[50]

Despite these limitations, JTF–4 appears to have improved counterdrug performnace. For the years 1991, 1992, and 1993, JTF–4 contributed over 50 percent of the total cocaine seized by law enforcement agencies.[51] It is difficult to measure the impact and efficiency of JTF–4, or to compare its performance with the other task forces. Prior to the creation of ONDCP, government-wide statistics for drug seizures were not compiled, so it is hard to judge how much JTF–4 might have improved the national interdiction system. It is also difficult to compare JTF–4 with JTFs in other geographic areas. Data no longer exists that would let us compare drug seizures or budget, man, and machine hours by task force, and in any case the task forces operated under different circumstances. For example, JTF–4 was mostly concerned with disrupting cocaine shipments, while the Pacific region monitored by JTF–5 had a much greater heroin problem to contain.

JTF–4 not only made a significant contribution to improving U.S. counterdrug efforts and demonstrated the value of combining military and civilian counterdrug efforts, but it also revealed again the shortcomings of the lead agency approach. The support of DOD for counterdrug operations—a mission accepted grudgingly—was huge compared to the much more limited resources available to civilian law enforcement agencies. The expensive and sophisticated electronic command, control, and intelligence systems, aircraft, and ships that DOD provided greatly improved interdiction capabilities. However, with no dedicated assets of its own and no way of compelling cooperation from its force providers, JTF–4 was hamstrung by the whims of every organization that provided support. Limited law enforcement intelligence-sharing crippled the JTF–4 role as an intelligence fusion center and forced it to rely primarily on electronic assets owned by DOD for intelligence collection. Furthermore, JTF–4's two missions, intelligence fusion and drug interdiction, were largely kept separate, and there was none of the meshing of intelligence and operations that would later become a hallmark of JIATF–South. In sum, JTF–4 never really became a center for interagency collaboration. The military Services and law enforcement agencies cooperated in a limited sense while consistently putting their own organizational equities ahead of the counterdrug mission. However, an unexpected incentive was about to encourage more teamwork.

Austerity Spurs Innovation: NICCP 1993 and 1994

JTF–4 might have continued to slowly improve at its own pace, but the election of a new President, the signing of the North American Free Trade Agreement, and the death of Pablo Escobar signaled a reevaluation of the war on drugs.[52] The Clinton administration gave priority to drug rehabilitation treatment and to balancing the Federal budget. ONDCP was trimmed to barely 20 percent of what it had been under George H.W. Bush, and $211 million was cut from the Pentagon's budget for counterdrug operations for FY 1993.[53] At the same time, a review of counterdrug operations by the National Security Council led it to conclude that the drug war should be fought closer to the source countries.[54]

These changes led President Clinton on November 3, 1993, to sign Presidential Decision Directive 14 (PDD–14). Whereas previous supply-side counterdrug operations (including the

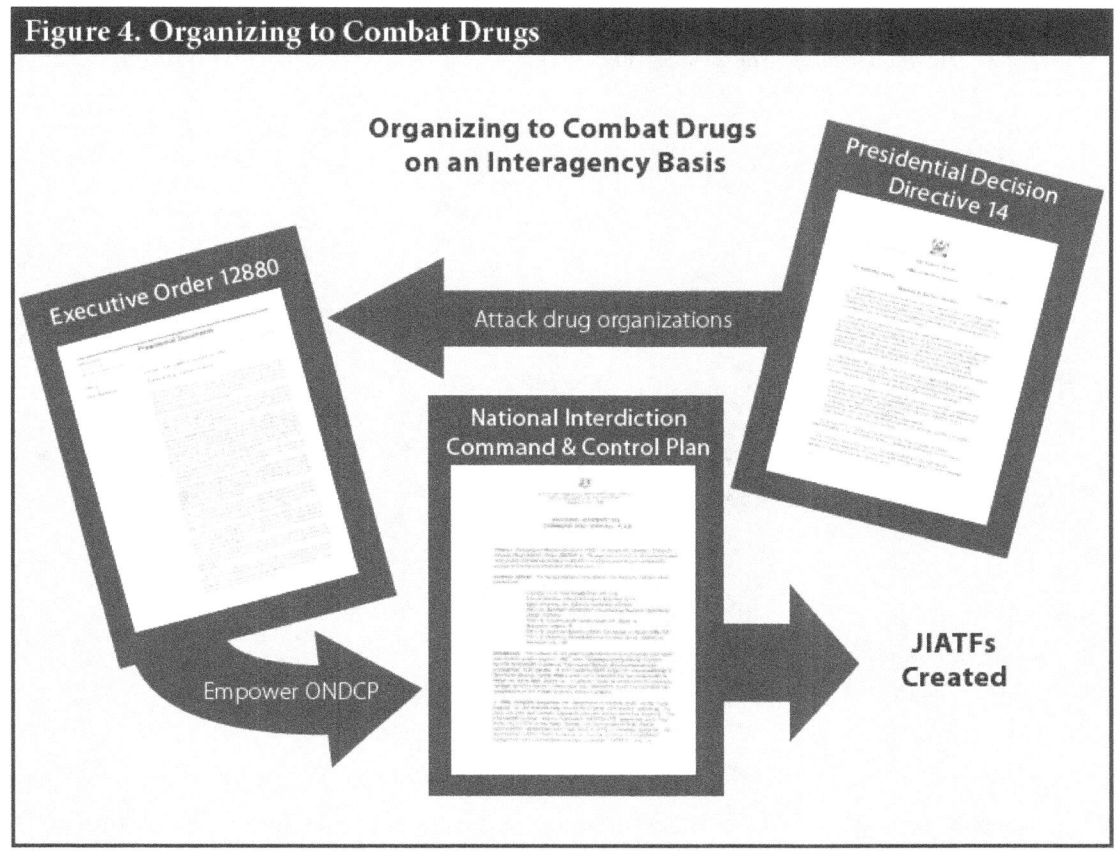

Figure 4. Organizing to Combat Drugs

Organizing to Combat Drugs on an Interagency Basis

Presidential Decision Directive 14

Executive Order 12880

Attack drug organizations

National Interdiction Command & Control Plan

Empower ONDCP

JIATFs Created

joint task forces) had focused on stopping drugs en route, PDD–14 shifted American focus to the source countries[55] and called for "providing assistance to those nations that show the political will to combat narco-trafficking through institution building . . . conducting efforts to destroy narco-trafficking organizations . . . [as well as] interdicting narcotics trafficking in both source countries and transit zones."[56] PDD–14 contained two other important items. It instructed the director of ONDCP to appoint a Coordinator for Drug Interdiction who would "ensure that assets dedicated by the Federal drug program agencies for interdiction are sufficient and that their use is properly integrated and optimized." It also ordered a review of U.S. counternarcotics command and control intelligence centers, including the JTFs.[57]

Signed 13 days later, Executive Order 12880 followed up on PDD–14 by strengthening ONDCP. It made the director of ONDCP responsible for reviewing and certifying[58] the budgets of all Federal agencies and departments to ensure their support of the the National Drug Control Strategy. PDD–14 also charged ONDCP with making suggestions for how to streamline the drug war and increase cooperation between agencies. It further made ONDCP responsible for

Coast Guard Cutter *Tahoma* crewmembers offloaded 88 bales (5,700 pounds) of cocaine with an estimated street value of more than $80 million

USCG (Nick Ameen)

developing metrics to measure drug supply and availability as well as to determine the success of the counterdrug effort. ONDCP also became responsible for "oversight and direction of all international counternarcotics policy development and implementation." It also reiterated the PDD–14 requirements for a reassessment of the counternarcotics command and control and intelligence centers and the appointment of an interagency coordinator for drug interdiction.[59] These measures gave the director of ONDCP the responsibility for providing oversight, direction, and coordination to all Federal agencies involved in the drug war. Paradoxically, however, it did not give the director of ONDCP enough authority to compel cooperation between agencies. On January 25, 1994, the ONDCP position was marginally strengthened by the *Violent Crime Control and Law Enforcement Act of 1994*, which allowed ONDCP to review department and agency budget requests for compliance with the "National Drug Control Strategy" and granted ONDCP the right to temporarily move people from one agency to another to create counterdrug task forces.[60]

Based on these new authorities and a review of the JTFs, the director of ONDCP distributed the first National Interdiction Command and Control Plan (NICCP) on April 7, 1994. The NICCP created a new model for drug interdiction: the Joint Interagency Task Force (JIATF). With the stroke of a pen, C³I Centers East and West were disestablished, JTF–4 became JIATF–

East, and JTF–5 became JIATF–West. JTF–South, a joint task force in Panama City owned by USSOUTHCOM, which had theretofore only been peripherally involved in drug interdiction, became JIATF–South. JIATF–South would focus on source country initiatives and the detection and monitoring of suspect drug targets for subsequent handoff to either participating national law enforcement agencies or to JIATF–East for further monitoring.[61] JIATF–East also took on the international air detection and monitoring responsibilities from the now defunct C³I Center East. Lastly, a Domestic Air Interdiction Coordination Center was also established, which assumed the domestic air sorting and response role formerly owned by both C³I Centers.[62] Unlike the JTFs, which had been primarily military institutions, the new Joint Interagency Task Forces were intended to be interagency organizations. Although the JIATFs would remain inside the military chain of command, they were also designated as "national Task Forces." This allowed them to control assets from any department or agency.[63]

The NICCP was signed by DOD, the Coast Guard, and the Customs Service. These three organizations had, at one point or another, previously been charged as the lead agencies for either detection and monitoring or interdiction and arrest and were now obligated to fulfill their missions by working with the JIATFs. "The 'national' concept provided for an organizational structure which recognized the force multiplier effect that could be realized from a Task Force manned and led by personnel from the various agencies with a drug interdiction mission."[64] By implication, the physical assets these agencies were given by Congress for detection and monitoring purposes would now be put under the tactical control of the JIATFs, which would operate in discrete, nationally assigned geographic areas with detection and monitoring of illegal trafficking as their sole responsibility. The NICCP did not compel compliance from other agencies, but was widely perceived to imply that counternarcotics money given by Congress to agencies for detection and monitoring should be used in support of the JIATFs. These task forces would streamline detection and monitoring efforts by providing centralized planning, prioritization, coordination, and C⁴I for all agencies conducting detection and monitoring. The NICCP also gave the JIATFs the "power to consult," providing a national venue for cooperation and conferring legitimacy on efforts to coordinate with all other interested partners without seeking approval from higher authority.[65]

Early Years of the JIATFs: 1994 to 1998

The NICCP did not immediately improve counterdrug operations; in fact, for several years JIATF–East would disrupt less cocaine than it had in 1992. There were good reasons for this. Between 1989 and 1994, DOD threw considerable resources into counternarcotics. But in 1994, the Department committed to JIATF–East about half of the resources it had previously given JTF–4.[66] This decline reflected both a general drop in Defense expenditures for the drug war and DOD reluctance to finance a task force it no longer truly owned. JIATF–East and its partners also had to cope with an overall decline in funding for transit zone drug interdiction, from a high of $1 billion in 1992 to $569 million in 1995.[67]

The end of the Soviet menace allowed DOD to deactivate a number of radar sites in the Caribbean between December 1994 and November 1995. Two Relocatable Over-the-Horizon Radars were dismantled and moved (one to Virginia and another to Texas). This type of radar was a major step forward in situational awareness, but it could not distinguish between legitimate and illegitimate aircraft. It also was poorly suited to vectoring interceptions; although it could see a wide area and detect suspicious flying behavior, it was hard to use the radar to pinpoint and track a trafficker's exact location. This made it difficult for JIATF–East to guide law enforcement vessels to the trafficker, making arrests and interdiction less likely.[68] Furthermore, JIATF–East still had few overseas human intelligence sources that could alert JIATF–East to coming drug shipments and "cue" the radar and other electronic intelligence systems to track particular vessels.[69] As a result, over the next few years, air seizures declined and maritime interceptions increasingly made up the bulk of cocaine disruptions by JIATF–East.[70]

The precipitous decline in Defense funding to support JIATF–East was not offset by funding and support from other agencies. The creation of the JIATFs assumed that:

> *full-time personnel assigned to the task forces would become stakeholders in their operations. It was anticipated that this would ensure close planning and operational coordination; the availability of Federal assets; and a seamless handoff of suspected air, sea, or land targets. Other agencies that either had an interest in or were impacted by the operations were to provide liaison personnel.[71]*

This did not happen, however. Agencies routinely failed to fully fill their designated staff billets in Key West. Although ONDCP and the U.S. interdiction coordinator had the authority to create and organize national interagency task forces, neither ONDCP nor the interdiction coordinator were given the authority to command the use of any agency's assets or personnel. JIATF–East and its partner task forces were composed of whatever staff and assets other agencies were willing to donate.[72] Customs, for example, filled only eight of the initial 22 staff positions it was given at JIATF–East, and some of these personnel lacked the necessary security

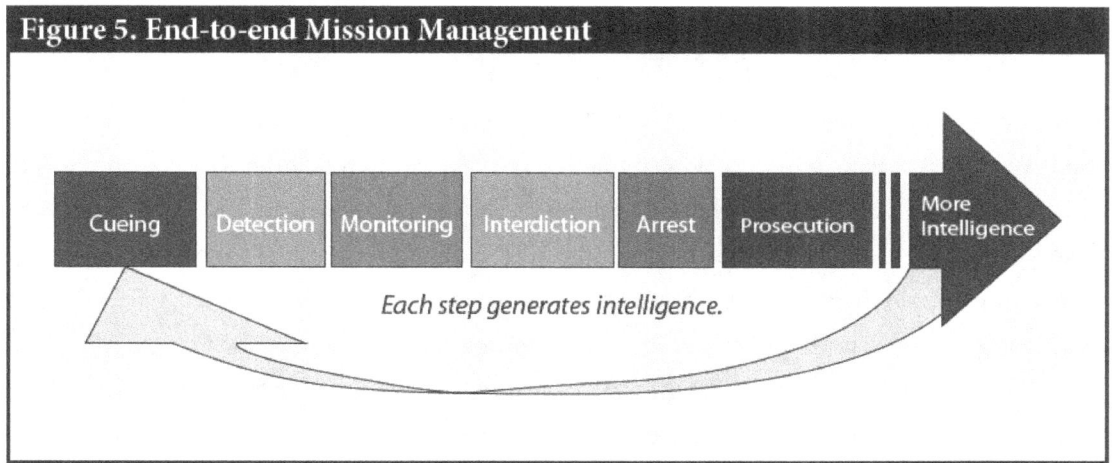

Figure 5. End-to-end Mission Management

Cueing · Detection · Monitoring · Interdiction · Arrest · Prosecution · More Intelligence

Each step generates intelligence.

clearances.[73] Even though DOD had cut much of its funding for counterdrug operations (particularly for ships and plans), it continued to supply the majority of personnel to JIATF–East.

JIATF–East also had trouble getting interdiction assets. It witnessed a more than 30 percent decline in ship days between 1992 and 1995, and in 1996 only half of all maritime traffickers JIATF–East monitored were interdicted or disrupted.[74] Traffickers who moved by air were even safer: only 26 of the 86 air events JIATF–East monitored led to successful cocaine disruptions. Not only was the Relocatable Over-the-Horizon Radar poorly suited for locating and vectoring air events, but JIATF–East's efforts were hampered by its limited access to Airborne Early Warning (AEW) equipped assets, which would have given it a great advantage over airborne traffickers.[75] Even on occasions when DEA agents could get good intelligence on air routes and JIATF–East had the AEW assets to monitor them, JIATF–East did not have the right assets for interdiction. Traffickers would "throw our guys the bird out the window knowing they could fly safely."[76]

There were also significant impediments to JIATF–East's intelligence collection mission. A major review of counterdrug support programs shortly after the creation of the JIATFs concluded that counterdrug intelligence collection was hampered by "(1) legal and agency-imposed limitations on access to law enforcement intelligence, (2) limited predictive analysis, and (3) problems of host nation corruption. Available intelligence information was not considered timely or specific enough regarding locations to support successful operations." As a result, ONDCP promulgated the Interdiction Intelligence Support Plan in March 1995 to ensure that the JIATF–South, the Domestic Air Interdiction Control Center, the Intelligence Analysis Center, and the U.S. Customs Service National Aviation Center were given access to necessary intelligence.[77] However, this decree doesn't appear to have had any effect.

JIATF–East's job got tougher as its area of operations expanded. On June 1, 1997, the US-SOUTHCOM area of responsibility expanded to include the Caribbean, and thus JIATF–East. This change was reflected in the September 17, 1997, revisions to the National Interdiction Command and Control Plan, which stipulated that JIATF–East was to remain in Key West but would add the Eastern Pacific and Central America to its area of responsibility. JIATF–East was now tasked with the "detection, monitoring, sorting, and handoff of suspect air and maritime drug-trafficking events in the Pacific Ocean east of 92 west longitude, the Gulf of Mexico, the Caribbean Sea, Central America north of Panama, and surrounding seas and the Atlantic Ocean."[78]

Soon thereafter, USSOUTHCOM was obliged to leave Panama by December 31, 1999, in compliance with the Panama Canal Treaties, which called for the return to Panama of territory held by the United States. USSOUTHCOM moved to Miami and JIATF–South, which had also been located at Howard Air Force Base in Panama City, merged with JIATF–East in Key West. JIATF–East and JIATF–South each had about 250 people, but many of the JIATF–South staff were double-hatted, working for both USSOUTHCOM headquarters and JIATF–South.[79] Because these staff members were important for the functioning of USSOUTHCOM and because budget restrictions limited the size of JIATF–East, only a handful of personnel from JIATF–South ended up in JIATF–East. Thus, JIATF–East's expanded responsibilities were not matched with a commensurate augmentation of staff with institutional knowledge of its new area of operations.[80] This shortcoming was further complicated by the difficulty of assimilating inter-agency partners (particularly the Customs Service and its flight of P–3s) into JIATF–East. It would take several years before JIATF–East gained the trust of its new partners and learned how to best use the capabilities they offered.[81] During this period of transition USSOUTHCOM decided to pull the budget and personnel functions from JIATF–East to consolidate them at USSOUTHCOM headquarters. The move was interpreted by some as an attempt by the command to tighten its control over JIATF–East, which kept relations between USSOUTHCOM and JIATF–East tense for a few years afterwards.[82]

JIATF–East Lays the Foundation for JIATF–South: 1999 to 2003

The merger of JIATF–East and JIATF–South, completed by May 1, 1999, did present one notable advantage for interdiction operations. Previously, JIATF–South had been responsible for counterdrug operations in the source countries and was supposed to use the intelligence it gathered to alert JIATF–East to potential drug shipments so that JIATF–East could monitor and interdict them. However, this division of labor represented an "organizational blink" in which information on drug trafficking could be lost or responses delayed. By bringing

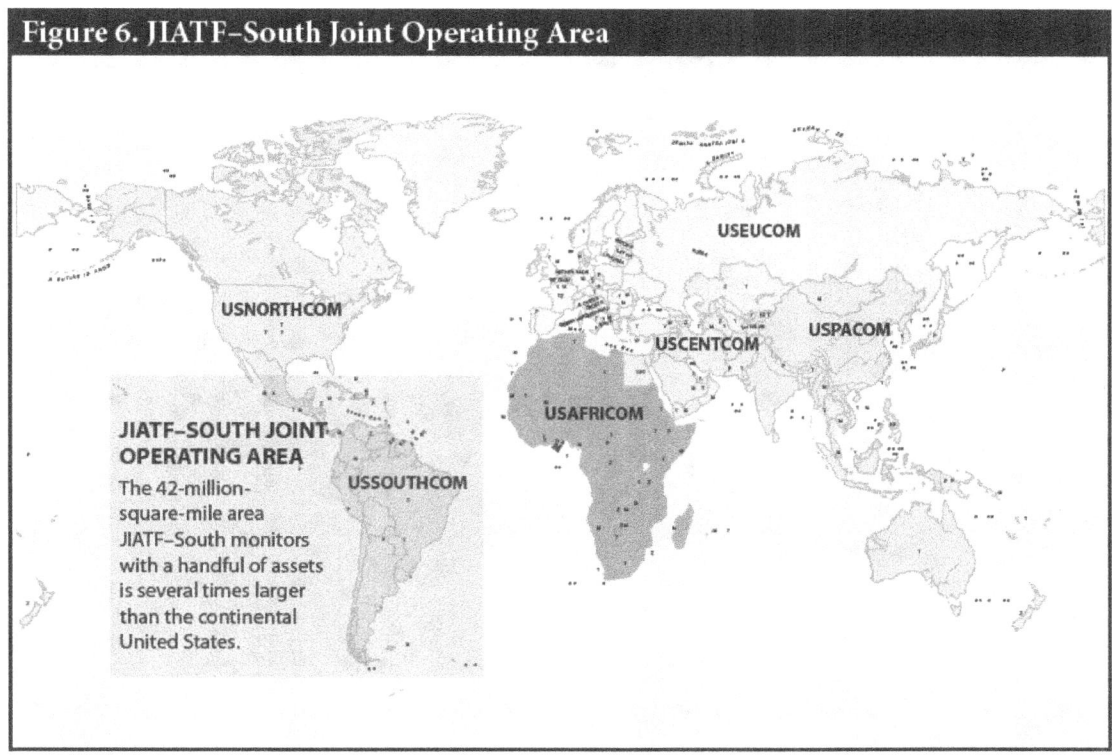

Figure 6. JIATF–South Joint Operating Area

USEUCOM

USNORTHCOM

USCENTCOM

USPACOM

USAFRICOM

JIATF–SOUTH JOINT OPERATING AREA

The 42-million-square-mile area JIATF–South monitors with a handful of assets is several times larger than the continental United States.

USSOUTHCOM

together the responsibilities and intelligence assets that had previously been divided between the two organizations, JIATF–East could create a more holistic picture of trafficking, watching drugs from the moment they were harvested until they hit U.S. shores. JIATF–East also gained tactical control over some of the air assets previously used by JIATF–South. The planes that could no longer be stationed at Howard Air Force Base in Panama were now sent to Forward Operating Locations in Ecuador, El Salvador, Aruba, and Curacao, giving them better coverage of JIATF–East's new area of responsibility.[83]

By 1999, JIATF–East had also become much better at accomplishing its mission of "'maximiz[ing] the disruption of drug transshipment,' collecting, integrating and disseminating intelligence, and guiding detection and monitoring forces for tactical action."[84] It significantly improved its intelligence collection, spurred by the downturn in counterdrug budgets. Between 1992 and 1999, DOD contributions to JIATF–East declined by 68 percent for flight hours and 62 percent for ship days.[85] Limited resources meant that JIATF–East could no longer afford to blindly search for smugglers. Instead, it had to do a much better job at using both human and electronic intelligence to cue its assets for detection and monitoring as well as interdiction. Better intelligence on smuggling routes from source countries allows ships and

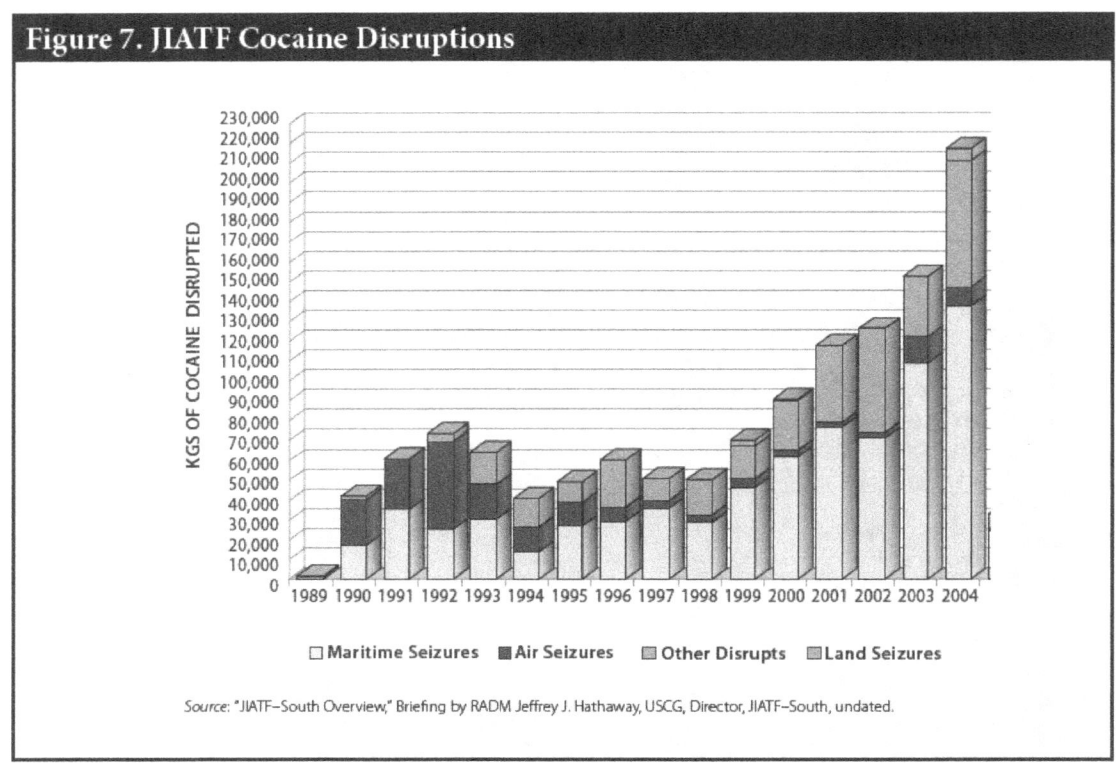

Figure 7. JIATF Cocaine Disruptions

Source: "JIATF–South Overview," Briefing by RADM Jeffrey J. Hathaway, USCG, Director, JIATF–South, undated.

planes to be prepositioned to intercept smugglers. Cueing also helped sort real targets from all the electronic chatter created by the thousands of legitimate vessels plying the oceans. Admiral Robert E. Kramek explained the new approach to Congress, "Where we would have [had] defense in depth with many assets and perhaps using 15 or 20 percent intelligence, we now rely on intelligence for over 80 percent of our operations so that we can focus on what we really know, because we don't have extra aircraft time or radar time or ship time."[86] The improvements in intelligence fusion meant that JIATF–South could put together tactical products that operators could use to great effect.[87]

Intelligence came from many sources. JIATF–East used the Domestic Air Interdiction Co-ordination Center, Customs' primary detection and monitoring organization, to "sort aircraft as they depart source and transit nations to identify suspect drug smuggling aircraft coming toward the eastern United States." It also used the Imagery Exploitation Section of the Coast Guard Intelligence Center for tactical and strategic imagery intelligence.[88] The Collections Management Division at JIATF–East, which worked on developing intelligence programs for cueing the detection and monitoring assets, also contained an imagery exploitation cell. In addition, the National Security Agency gave JIATF–East a Cryptologic Services Group that provided it with direct signals intelligence support.[89] By 1998, the 76-person JIATF–East Intelligence Directorate far exceeded the Intelligence Directorates of JIATF–South and JIATF–West, with respectively 19 and 33 persons.[90]

Two particular intelligence programs were emerging that would pay rich rewards in the coming years, Panama Express and the tactical analysis teams. In 1999, the United States was able to convert José Castrillón Henao, the "movement coordinator" for Pablo Escobar, into an informer (see sidebar on page 26).[91] Castrillón Henao was an intelligence bonanza. Reportedly, he could simply read a selection of ship manifests and immediately know which ones were smugglers and where they were likely to go. He provided so much information that law enforcement officials decided to build an interagency "organized crime drug enforcement Task Force" around him, named Panama Express in honor of his expedited entrance into the United States.[92] Panama Express proved to be an unbelievably productive intelligence source, especially when paired with JIATF–East's assets. The relationship between the two organizations was nurtured through a personal relationship. The extraordinary FBI agent who ran Panama Express had previously lived next door to the director of JIATF–East and trusted him to protect the Panama Express source. For its part, JIATF–East provided Panama Express with funding, analysts, computers, and liaison officers,[93] and later a secure phone and computer network that replaced the need for liaisons.

The second source of intelligence came from the burgeoning use of tactical analysis teams based in foreign countries. Although JTF–4 and JIATF–East had put liaison officers on Embassy Country Teams in South America for a decade, agents located overseas became an increasingly important source of information for JIATF–East. Tactical analysis teams are generally located inside American Embassies or Consulates and consist of one to three JIATF–East intelligence officers who worked on a day-to-day basis supporting law enforcement agencies resident in the Embassy, especially the DEA country attaché. However, the tactical analysis teams are ultimately managed and funded by the JIATF–East Intelligence Directorate[94] and directly represented the director, JIATF–East within the U.S. Ambassador's Country Team.[95] By being overseas, the tactical analysis teams gave JIATF–East much more information than would typically filter back indirectly to Key West from Country Teams. They also plugged into a network of downrange counterdrug intelligence sources[96] and provided "unique insights [into] the nuances of each Country Team as well as cultural and language sensitivity which enhance[s] effective coordination with allies."[97] The tactical analysis teams proved valuable but initially required some remedial work. USSOUTHCOM gave JIATF–East control over the command's tactical analysis teams after it merged with JIATF–South in part

Panama Express

An unmatchable source of counterdrug intelligence became available in 1999 in the form of José Castrillón Henao, the "movement coordinator" for Pablo Escobar. Splitting his time between Panama and Colombia, Castrillón Henao coordinated the movement of money and drugs throughout Latin America and the United States, primarily through a tuna fishing company he set up in Panama in 1989. Despite Escobar's end, Castrillón Henao kept his hands in the game and came under investigation by the Panamanian police after influencing the outcome of the Panamanian election in 1994 by contributing large amounts of money to the eventual winner, Ernesto Pérez Balladares. He also came to the attention of the Drug Enforcement Administration (DEA) and Central Intelligence Agency (CIA) after several of his fishing ships were found carrying large amounts of cocaine. The CIA went so far as to rent the apartment above his and drill holes through the ceiling so they could monitor his comings and goings. Panamanian police arrested him in 1996 for money laundering. He was put in prison, but in 1998, when a $1 million bribe was made for his release, the police hurriedly extradited him to the United States before it could happen. Landing in South Florida in May 1998, he agreed to cooperate with law enforcement officials in exchange for not spending any more time in jail.

Panama Express is an interagency team in its own right, and one that has proven to be a huge success. It has grown so much since its early days that it has split into two offices, Panama Express North and Panama Express South. These offices include representatives from the DEA, Federal Bureau of Investigation, Internal Revenue Service, U.S. Immigration and Customs Enforcement, U.S Coast Guard, U.S. Attorney for the Middle District of Florida, Florida Department of Law Enforcement, and the Sarasota, Hillsborough, and Pinellas Counties Sheriff's Offices. As with JIATF–South, the diversity at Panama Express brings great benefits: each agent brings to Panama Express a wealth of their own intelligence sources and contacts. This works symbiotically with knowledge gained from arrested smugglers to enable Panama Express to develop intelligence networks in South America. In the decade since its creation, its intelligence has led, by one count, to the disruption of 600 metric tons of cocaine and the successful prosecution of more than 1,300 smugglers. JIATF–South also works with many other law enforcement task forces such as those in Tampa, St. Petersburg, and Miami, Florida, and San Juan, Puerto Rico, which are all linked to JIATF–South by computer systems it provides.

because the teams faced severe personnel challenges, among them the need to weed out poor performers, including some who would later be arrested for various misdeeds including selling intelligence.[98]

JIATF–East's intelligence sources became increasingly important following the attacks on September 11, 2001. The rapid expansion of the Global War on Terror caused DOD to pull back many of the assets it usually provided to the JIATFs, particularly Navy ships and Air Force flying hours. The FBI also reconsidered its priorities after 9/11. The FBI's ability to commit personnel and resources to JIATF–East dwindled as it focused on counterterrorism. The Coast Guard, Customs Service, and international partners (particularly France, the Netherlands, and the United Kingdom)[99] picked up some of the slack, providing increased levels of planes and ships, partly compensating for this drawdown. The increasing use of armed Coast Guard helicopters also increased the "punch" of interdiction forces, allowing them to chase go-fasts and shoot out their engines, giving seaborne law enforcement detachments time to catch up and arrest the smugglers.[100] The DEA also increased its participation, which was particularly important as it had better overseas counterdrug intelligence networks than the FBI.[101] The JIATF–East electronic intelligence capabilities also expanded in 2003 after USSOUTHCOM merged the Joint Southern Surveillance and Reconnaissance Operation Center (JSSROC) with JIATF–East to increase efficiency and effectiveness. JSSROC had feeds covering the entire Caribbean as well as expansive signals intelligence capabilities that allowed JIATF–East to eavesdrop on smugglers, eventually forcing them to almost completely stop using electronic communication.[102] The JSSROC products were primarily used by JIATF–East.

By combining the human intelligence gleaned from DEA, tactical analysis teams, and Panama Express with a diverse array of electronic intelligence assets, JIATF–East could track drugs from the moment they were made until they were interdicted. Armed with knowledge of the drug shipment and its intended route, JIATF–East could electronically monitor vessels as they moved across the ocean and position its assets for interdiction. The arrested traffickers could then be brought back to Florida, prosecuted, and, in exchange for lenient sentencing, recruited to work for Panama Express, thus providing a fresh source of intelligence. "The intelligence led to very successful, predictable outcomes," recalled a former director. "We knew what was happening. There was no risk. We could put assets right where [the traffickers] would be. But there were repercussions. . . . A lot of our informants were killed."[103] In the following years, JIATF–East's growing intelligence fusion capacity would allow it to consistently do more interdiction with less detection and monitoring assets because it knew how best to position these assets to intercept smugglers.[104]

Coast Guardsmen keep a watchful eye on a smuggling go-fast boat with 58 bales of cocaine and four suspected smugglers on board

USCG (PA2 Donnie Brzuska)

The growing success of JIATF–East was acknowledged on October 1, 2003, when its area of responsibility was again expanded, this time moving farther into the Pacific. Expanding the JIATF–East area of responsibility in the Pacific had been talked about for years. Drug traffickers were swinging further out into the Pacific from the west coast of South America in order to avoid JIATF–East interdiction,[105] and JIATF–West, with its focus on heroin, had never concentrated on that area of its domain.[106] The percentage of drugs smuggled into the United States through the eastern Pacific shot up from 30 percent in the late 1990s to 60 percent by 2003.[107] Drug traffickers were again exploiting the organizational seam between JIATF–East and JIATF–West by moving back and forth between their areas of responsibilities to complicate continuous monitoring.[108] The traffickers exploited this boundary as much as possible, crossing it multiple times during a single trip to impede interdiction attempts.[109] This was a particularly troublesome issue in operations involving a foreign nation. For example, a long-running joint operation with Guatemala, "Mayan Jaguar," was ruined when a go-fast tracked by JIATF–East and the Guatemalans crossed into the JIATF–West area of responsibility:

> JIATF–East requested the JIATF–West ship to disengage and allow the Guatemalan's to intercept the target. JIATF–West did not comply and proceeded

with the intercept. As the target crossed the JIATF AOR [area of responsibility] boundary, the JIATF–West vessel intercepted first. JIATF–East requested a joint boarding, JIATF–West denied the request and effectively eliminat[ed] the Guatemalans [sic] role in the operation. The end result—while JIATF–West seized 2.4 metric tons of cocaine, the Guatemalans were quite angry over the incident and questioned the U.S. ability to keep to their agreements. Although the operation was a tactical success, it was a political failure and resulted in the Guatemalans withdrawing from joint counterdrug operations.[110]

In order to eliminate this problem, the operating areas for each JIATF were revised with USPACOM and USSOUTHCOM agreement, and with concurrence from all the interagency partners working with the JIATFs.[111] JIATF–East's area of responsibility was expanded into the eastern Pacific out to 120 degrees west. JIATF–East now owned 42 million square miles of operating area. This was a unique arrangement within DOD because it meant that although JIATF–East was subordinate to USSOUTHCOM, its area of operations extended into the operating areas of USPACOM and U.S. Northern Command (USNORTHCOM), as well as into U.S. European Command (USEUCOM) in the east. JIATF–West subsequently moved to Hawaii and refocused on building partner national police capabilities in the Far East.[112]

This latest expansion of JIATF–East's area of operations was another vote of confidence in JIATF–East and showed what a long way it had come in just under a decade. When the National Interdiction Command and Control Plan created JIATF–East, it was empowered as the sole authority for detection and monitoring operations within its operating area and with the express intent of handing off suspected traffickers to law enforcement forces. Without directly compelling interagency cooperation, this made Key West the obvious focal point for counterdrug efforts, as every agency with an interest in drugs would have to work through JIATF–East and use its detection and monitoring expertise to accomplish their own counterdrug missions. This did not happen immediately; it took interagency partners some time to see what a national interagency task force could do for them. Consequently, JIATF–East suffered through a period of poor performance as it adjusted to austerity, but it responded with a spurt of innovation. By improving its intelligence collection and fusion, JIATF–East more than compensated for its reduced assets. Intelligence improvements across a number of disciplines, but most importantly improvements in human intelligence, allowed the task force to make much better use of the limited assets it had by cueing them to incoming drug shipments.

As it improved and reached out to new partners, JIATF–East broadened its view of counterdrug operations from a focus on interdiction to "end-to-end" problem management. Rather than focusing simply on detection and monitoring as it previously had, JIATF–East now tracked the entire drug movement process: how bulk shipments were paid for in cash, stash areas, conveyances, off-loads and the follow-on movements. It also tracked who benefited from the shipment of drugs to include U.S. State Department–designated terrorist organizations, guns, munitions, and people of national interest. It followed the process until the smugglers were imprisoned, became informants, and began divulging intelligence that could lead to more interdictions and prosecutions. This breadth of view made JIATF–East a natural ally for every agency involved in counterdrug operations, which further improved performance. After a long evolution, JIATF–East finally had demonstrated that the whole-of-government approach to counternarcotics made it dramatically greater than the sum of its parts.

JIATF–South: The "Gold Standard" for Interagency Operations

Another indication of JIATF–East's growing reputation was the decision by the commander of USSOUTHCOM to change its name to JIATF–South so the two organizations would be more closely associated (this became effective April 23, 2003).[113] By the end of 2003, JIATF–South's effectiveness was attracting attention across the government. Substantiating the adage that "success breeds success," other organizations and countries increasingly sought out cooperative relationships with JIATF–South. Even though the task force faced a period of declining resources as assets were redirected to the Global War on Terror, continuing improvements in intelligence networks and operational practices allowed it to increase its success in interdictions and arrests. JIATF–South was soon reliably disrupting four times as much cocaine each year as had JTF–4 at its peak. Inside the U.S. Government, JIATF–South became *the* model for interagency collaboration as well as a widely cited example of effective intelligence fusion. Then, as now, it attracted thousands of visitors each year, including department and agency heads. JIATF–South has earned many admirers, but few who have been able to emulate its success. To better explain its performance and assess the extent to which it can be replicated, it is necessary to delve more deeply into the attributes that typically explain high performing cross-functional, interagency teams. (In the discussion that follows, we will refer to all previous manifestations of the organization as JIATF–South to avoid constantly distinguishing between specific time periods and different organizational names, all of which were covered in the previous historical overview.)

Performance Variables

To better assess why JIATF–South works so well, we have examined its performance using 10 variables drawn from the organization and management literature on cross-functional

Table 1. Milestones in JIATF–South Organizational History

Event	Impact
National Security Decision Directive 221, 1986	President Reagan declares narcotrafficking a national security threat and authorizes U.S. military forces to support the counterdrug mission.
The Anti-Drug Abuse Act of 1988 (PL100–690)	Congress created the Office of National Drug Control Policy (ONDCP) in the Executive Office of the President to coordinate the war on drugs.
National Defense Authorization Act for Fiscal Year 1989	Congress designated the Department of Defense (DOD) the lead agency for the detection and monitoring of drug trafficking into the United States, and the Coast Guard as the lead agency for the interdiction and arrest of drug traffickers.
JTF–4, April 1989	A DOD organizational construct proves the value of greater military participation in the war on drugs, but also that it could not forge an interagency effort even as the designated lead agency. Multiple organizations had their own intelligence collection and assessment efforts; their own targeting priorities; their own command, control, and communication procedures and systems; their own operational picture; and unilaterally employed their assets as they saw fit.
Presidential Decision Directive 14 and Executive Order 12880, 1993	President Clinton's counterdrug strategy shifts the focus to source countries and attacking narcotrafficking organizations. It also strengthened ONDCP, giving its director responsibility for recommending improvements to organizational structure and for certifying the budgets of all Federal agencies and departments to ensure their support of the National Drug Control Strategy.
NICCP, April 7, 1994	Using his new authorities, the Director of ONDCP disseminates the first National Interdiction Command and Control Plan (NICCP). The NICCP replaced DOD's Joint Task Forces with Joint Interagency Task Forces (JIATFs), which were to be considered "national task forces."
JIATF–South merged with JIATF–East, 1999	In compliance with the 1979 Panama Canal Treaty, JIATF–South leaves Panama and is relocated in Key West, Florida, where it merges with JIATF–East. JIATF–East's productivity continues to climb.
Joint Operating Area established, 2003	JIATF–East's area of operations was expanded into the Eastern Pacific out to 120 degrees west so traffickers can no longer exploit organizational seams between JIATF–West and JIATF–East.
Panama Express, 2000	José Castrillón Henao becomes an FBI informant in 1999, and his information enables a law enforcement task force—Panama Express—to better fight the Colombian drug cartels. JIATF–South forges a productive partnership with Panama Express the following year.
JIATF–East is renamed JIATF–South, April 25, 2003	The change more closely aligned the JIATF's name to its geographic area of responsibility, but also was a strong indication of the organization's growing reputation for operational success.

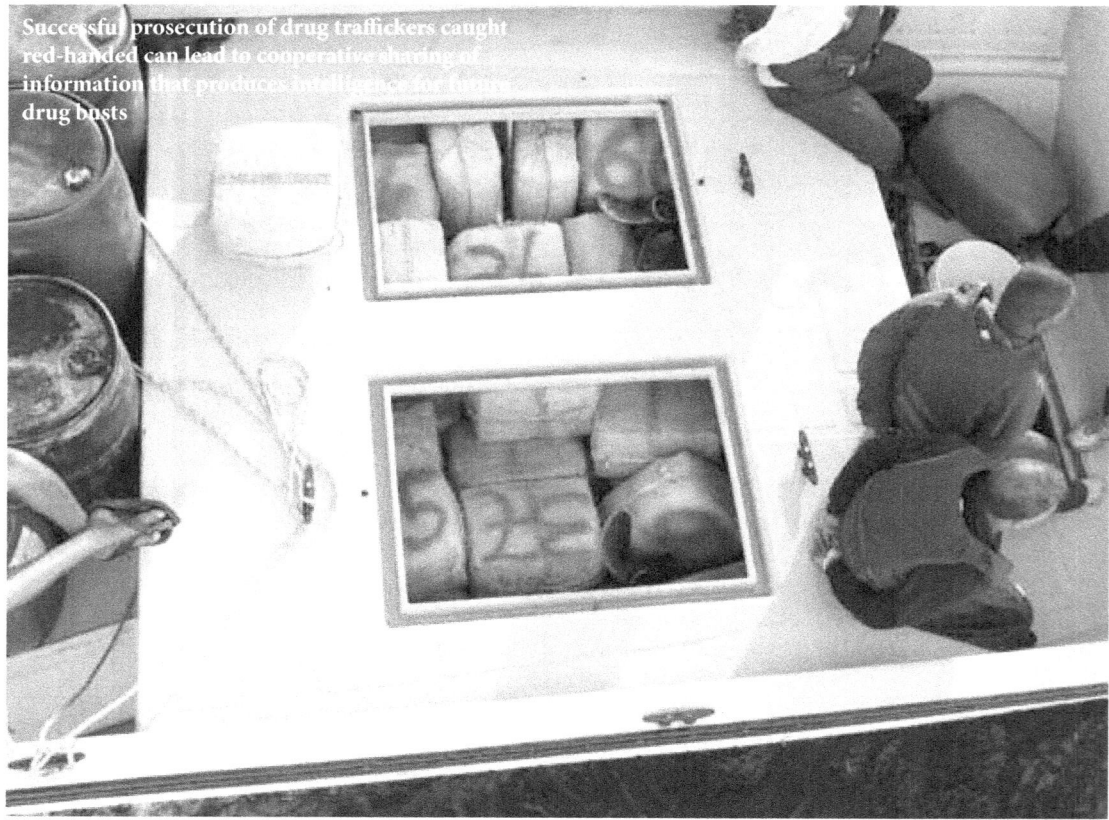

Successful prosecution of drug traffickers caught red-handed can lead to cooperative sharing of information that produces intelligence for future drug busts

teams.[114] All 10 variables are attributes of the team, but we group them by their scope, beginning with three organizational-level variables: purpose, empowerment, and organizational context. We then consider team-level variables: structure, decisionmaking, culture, and learning. Finally, we assess variables at the level of the individual team members: team composition, rewards, and leadership.

The effect of these three sets of variables may be likened to a sailing vessel. The wind and weather are organizational-level variables that determine the conditions the team operates under and to some extent what direction it can move. The team-level variables are the ship itself, providing the team's basic operational structure and mechanisms. The individual-level characteristics are, like the ship's crew, microdeterminants of performance that occasionally have a major performance impact, for better or worse.

We provide a brief explanation of each variable and then assess its importance in explaining the success of JIATF–South. We focus on understanding the task force's performance between 2004 and the present, and in particular on understanding its leadership team. The

Table 2. Performance Variables

Level	Variables	Defined
Organization	Purpose	The broad, long-term mandate given to the team by its management as well as the alignment of short-term objectives with the strategic vision and agreement on common approaches within the team.
	Empowerment	Access to sufficient high-quality personnel, funds, and materials, and an appropriate amount of authority that allows for confident, decisive action.
	Support	The set of organizational processes that connect a team to other teams at multiple levels within the organization, other organizations, and a wide variety of resources the team needs to accomplish its mission.
Team	Structure	The "mechanics" of teams—design, collocation, and networks—that affect team productivity.
	Decisionmaking	The mechanisms that are employed to make sense of and solve a variety of complex problems faced by a cross-functional team.
	Culture	The shared values, norms and beliefs of the team—behavioral expectations and level of commitment and trust among team members.
	Learning	An ongoing process of reflection and action through which teams acquire, share, combine, and apply knowledge.
Individual	Composition	What individual members bring to the group in terms of skill, ability, and disposition.
	Rewards	Material incentives and psychological rewards to direct team members towards the accomplishment of the team's mission.
	Leadership	The collection of strategic actions that are taken to accomplish team objectives, to ensure a reasonable level of efficiency, and to avoid team catastrophes.

Source: For further discussion of the variables, see James Douglas Orton with Christopher J. Lamb, "Interagency National Security Teams: Can Social Science Contribute?" *PRISM* 2, no. 2 (Washington, DC: National Defense University Press, March 2011).

leadership team nominally consists of its "command group" and J-Staff leads, but may expand to include other relevant parties for particular decisions, including foreign liaison officers stationed at JIATF–South to coordinate their country's participation in counterdrug efforts. The key attributes that explain JIATF–South's performance today were initiated or instituted by the organization's leadership team, even if many aspects of its performance are a normal part of its organizational routine. Descriptions of leadership team experiences were consistent, although interviewees sometimes differed in how they assessed the relative importance of some variables.

Organizational-level Variables

JIATF–South does not exist in a vacuum, nor do other cross-functional teams. Much of a team's effectiveness is attributable to exogenous factors[115] related to the broader organization or system within which it operates. Typically, a team's purpose, degree of empowerment, and level of organizational support are dependent upon its broader organizational milieu. Before a team is created, some higher authority usually determines what it should accomplish (purpose), whether it will be subordinate or superior to other parts of the organization, and from whence its resources will come (empowerment). Depending on the broader organization's approach to teams, there also will be varying levels of support offered to them. These organizational-level variables constitute the "fertile soil" in which the team must grow. Thus, they have a major impact on team effectiveness.

1. *Team purpose.* A strong sense of purpose unifies a team and provides direction.[116] This is certainly the case at JIATF–South. Its mission to combat illegal trafficking is clearly understood. As the director of the task force told Congress in 2005, "There is no ambiguity in what we are charged to do."[117] Initially, however, JIATF–South construed its counternarcotics mission so narrowly that it undermined interagency collaboration. Under DOD and Coast Guard leadership, the organization focused too narrowly on "detecting and monitoring" drug shipments, especially on the high seas. Patrolling operations were scheduled, and any available intelligence that might support the patrols was requested. Legal restrictions on use of DOD assets for law enforcement also encouraged this narrow conceptualization of the mission. Yet law enforcement organizations had little incentive to partner with the JIATF if the mission did not include prosecuting criminals.

Over time, JIATF–South leaders broadened their understanding of the organization's mission, adopting an end-to-end conceptualization of the problem. The organization partnered with law enforcement and embassies to develop intelligence sources in the producing countries that would help cue monitoring and detection of drug shipments. It also partnered with customs and law enforcement to ensure drug seizures were handled in a manner that would lead to successful prosecutions, more informers, and more intelligence on drug organization activities. A consensus developed that intelligence drove operations and had to be given priority—particularly protecting sources. The close "intel-ops fusion" and the benefits of attacking the cocaine-producing organizations in all phases of their operations constitute a broad "shared mental model" that deepens the sense of purpose for JIATF–South personnel.

When JIATF–South adopted an end-to-end understanding of its mission, the entire interagency team could support it.[118] Every partnering agency agrees that combating illegal trafficking is important (and something for which they have been given funding by Congress).[119] The mission is discrete and well understood and helps the agencies achieve their organizational goals.[120] A strong shared purpose motivates team members to transcend the competing cultures of their home agencies and helps unify the efforts of people with very different backgrounds and experiences.[121] It is the "cement" that holds the team together when inevitable differences of opinion arise. For this reason, leaders make sure the mission is "sold continuously and folks . . . buy in to why they are there."[122]

New arrivals at Key West usually do not have joint military or interagency experience, and often begin with a more limited view of the JIATF–South mission. With time they adopt a more holistic view,[123] often coming to see themselves as at war with the drug organizations and fighting them all the way through the trafficking process from production to delivery in the United States. Many members see their mission as support to law enforcement, with the customer being the prosecutor who nails the trafficker.[124] An even broader perspective was offered by a JIATF–South intelligence director who noted that although as a new team member he saw the task force as an American organization working for American ends to prevent drugs from entering the United States, he later came to believe the deeper purpose was to gather evidence on traffickers that could be delivered to foreign nations so the traffickers could be arrested and prosecuted by other nations: "We weren't there to support the two star; we were there to support the foreign officers . . . the whole system was geared to doing this and to taking very restricted information and getting it to the right people."[125] Because of the complexity of the war on drugs, JIATF–South leaders realized that the organization could not accomplish its mission of preventing drugs from entering the United States simply through interdiction. Traffickers can increase production and diversify delivery in response to JIATF–South's increasingly effective interdiction efforts. The majority of their shipments will get through in any case. Thus JIATF–South leaders realized they could not "seize their way to success" but instead had "to get the guys who orchestrate" the drug shipments.[126]

JIATF–South's sense of purpose is actually more sharply focused than the combating illegal trafficking mission suggests.[127] The task force focuses almost exclusively on counternarcotics, and on cocaine in particular. In the post-9/11 environment, JIATF–South is encouraged to interpret illegal trafficking more broadly, and it accordingly pays greater attention to potential terrorists transiting U.S. borders. However, JIATF–South is still focused on what it knows best, what its fragile coalition of partners signed up for, and what it is funded to do,[128] which is to combat cocaine trafficking. This strong sense of purpose is unanimously cited as highly motivating and a critical factor in the organization's success. For many, it is unique compared to the rest of their government experience.[129]

2. *Empowerment (authority and resources).* In order for a team to perform well, it must be empowered with the authority and resources necessary to fulfill its purpose and accomplish its mission. If the team is given authority and control of the resources it needs to succeed—including time, skills, and information[130]—it can be held accountable for success or failure. Because of the way government is structured and resourced, it is common to approve interagency strategies without empowering the people or organizations charged with their execution, which contributes to a certain amount of cynicism. One senior government official spoke for many when he noted "vision without resources is a hallucination."[131] JIATF–South, however, is fortunate to be well empowered for its mission. Perhaps most important, it has been able to obtain the resources required for its mission in a variety of ways.

Congress provides separate counterdrug funds to the departments and agencies. JIATF–South's requests for funds and its operating budget flow through DOD, and specifically through USSOUTHCOM. Whatever funding Congress provides is then put in a DOD counternarcotics central transfer account, which ensures that money intended for the task force is not touched by any other organization.[132] JIATF–South's budget requests are also overseen by both the Counter-Narcotics Office in the Office of the Secretary of Defense as well as the ONDCP, both advocates for sufficient counterdrug funding. ONDCP in particular is charged with ensuring appropriate levels of funding for national counterdrug priorities, although it prefers to proceed cooperatively rather than contend with powerful departments and agencies.[133] DOD was, in the words of one JIATF–South director, "dragged kicking and screaming" into the war on drugs, but historically its support has been critical. The Department provides consistent budgetary support,[134] funding the headquarters, its operations and some assets, equipment, and training.[135]

JIATF–South cobbles together its operational assets from multiple sources, however. Other organizations contribute planes and ships to operations that JIATF–South plans and runs. The NICCP stipulates that the Department of Homeland Security and DOD are to provide appropriate support to JIATF–South, "but it's always a struggle to get what one needs on time."[136] To facilitate the asset allocation process, JIATF–South hosts a semiannual planning conference that brings together all its counterdrug partners. The interagency and international partners review their efforts from the past 3 months, plan for new initiatives and combined operations, and decide what assets they want to give the task force for the next 6 to 9 months, usually by calculating the number of airplane hours and ship days.[137] The NICCP requires JIATF–South to provide an annual statement of need to force providers. In turn, the Departments of Defense and of Homeland Security are supposed to coordinate their resource allocation and respond with a statement of intent to provide assets. In the past, both Departments sometimes failed to provide the requested information, but that has changed in recent years.[138] While the NICCP requires those U.S. organizations providing forces to coordinate with JIATF–South, their contributions are voluntary, as are the international contributions.[139] Task force leaders do not try to codify agreements with force providers in memoranda of understanding. They understand JIATF–South can't "create a lot of paperwork and hold their feet to the fire"[140] because it would just cause others to shy away and make lesser commitments.[141] Working without written agreements allows for great flexibility in problem-solving. Any agency can walk away from verbal commitments made to JIATF–South any time it wants, but the civilian agencies at least tend to meet their commitments or even provide more support than they promised. DOD and the Coast Guard are more likely to have to pull assets away for other national emergencies or contingencies.

Partnering agencies thus retain operational control of their assets, but as the NICCP stipulates, JIATF–South is given tactical control over the units that parent agencies furnish (along with the personnel and funds to operate them). This means that it can move assets around its operating area like chess pieces. It has to assemble an appropriate "force package" of ships and aircraft from different interagency and international partners for every mission, which is a considerable challenge. There are other drawbacks to the "coalition of the willing" approach as well. For example, long-term planning is impossible, and JIATF–South is less flexible in responding to new threats because it is uncertain whether the necessary assets will be made available.[142] This resourcing method also means there will be shortfalls during emergencies such as Hurricane Katrina or the Gulf oil spill, when the Coast Guard and other agencies have to redirect their forces to deal with higher priorities.[143] It is noteworthy, however, that when DOD pulled back operational assets during the 1990s, and again after 9/11, JIATF–South was able to respond well to the austerity. In the 1990s, it expanded its concept of operations and attracted more law enforcement support, and more recently it has added international partners and expanded other forms of cooperation.

Another form of resource cooperation that JIATF–South exploits is research and development partnerships. Since it has a real-world action mission that is nonlethal for the

JIATF–South partners with Pennsylvania State University, the U.S. Navy, and Office of Secretary Defense Rapid Release of Technology Office to evaluate an advanced unmanned underwater vehicle that can detect and monitor highly mobile objects

most part, this task force is an attractive test bed for new technologies. In fact, the National Security Agency, National Reconnaissance Office, National Geospatial-Intelligence Agency, and Central Intelligence Agency have designated it a "tactical live environment test bed to test and evaluate current and emerging technologies against highly mobile dark asymmetrical threats."[144] JIATF–South leaders have found that other agencies will provide them both money and material to test new technologies during counterdrug operations.[145] It has "the best toys money can buy" since it is "the perfect test bed for non-lethal technologies."[146] A recent example is the testing of the "Stiletto," a high-speed, low-cost vessel designed for use in riverine and littoral operations.[147] JIATF–South is an ideal nonlethal environment for experimenting with "anything and everything DOD might want."[148] Research and development funding also comes from the Defense Advanced Research Projects Agency and the intelligence agencies, who see similarities between counterdrug operations and other missions such as counterterrorism, and who value a real-world but reasonably safe arena to test new programs. This money usually goes directly to the budgets of the Intelligence or Operations Directorates, for whom outside funding may comprise a significant portion of their annual budget.[149] Such funding is ad hoc and typically provided on the basis of a handshake rather than being formally programmed.[150] JIATF–South has a reputation for using such funds well, demonstrating that it is flexible and innovative and can get results. Success thus keeps the funds coming, but the donating organization is still in control and is not obligated to provide them. In addition to these traditional sources of funding, JIATF–South and similar organizations that perform mutually supportive counterdrug and counterterror operations can now draw money from both funding pools[151] under certain conditions.[152]

JIATF–South's directive authority is a mix of top-down congressional and executive branch mandates and negotiated outcomes. After experimenting with various lead agency approaches in the 1980s proved ineffective, Congress and the executive branch decided fighting drugs was a national priority that demanded a national response.[153] Declaring drugs a national security problem brought DOD support to the table and led to the creation of the national task forces, with implied authority to coordinate across departments and agencies. More important, the National Interdiction Command and Control Plan makes JIATF–South the sole agent that can perform detection and monitoring within its 42-million-square-mile operating area. This singular responsibility makes the task force the natural focal point for intelligence fusion and reduces the problem of multiple agencies with competing jurisdictions.[154] Other organizations are under pressure to cooperate with it, and JIATF–South leaders have skillfully used their authorities and reputation to create a collaborative enterprise that is truly greater than the sum of its parts.

With so many agencies cooperating, JIATF–South has access to a potent package of legal authorities.[155] What one component does not have authority to do, another has. For example, DOD cannot make arrests or conduct criminal investigations, but other partners can. Along with its tactical control of other agencies' assets during operations, these diverse authorities mean that JIATF–South does not "have to ask 'mother may I' when chasing smugglers."[156] When law enforcement officials are about to interdict or arrest traffickers, tactical control is shifted to the appropriate U.S. Coast Guard law enforcement authority (Coast Guard District Seven in Miami, Florida, or District Eleven in Alameda, California; see sidebar on page 40). If the Coast Guard law enforcement officers are on board the U.S. or partner nation naval vessel, the vessel will actually take down its own flag and fly the U.S. Coast Guard flag, at which point the senior law enforcement officer exercises the Coast Guard's law enforcement authority until the case is concluded.[157]

JIATF–South's success inclines observers to assume it has some unique national authority to control assets and resources from diverse executive departments and agencies.[158] In reality, its de jure authority is relatively weak. The Office of National Drug Control Policy can advocate

Anatomy of an Interagency Counterdrug Interdiction[1]

When JIATF–South's detection and monitoring operations have progressed to the point where it is clear that a law enforcement action will take place, tactical control of the detection and monitoring asset—usually ships—is handed over to law enforcement. To illustrate, a U.S. Navy ship is conducting detection and monitoring operations under the tactical control of JIATF–South. After a sorting process by JIATF–South and in cooperation with all of its partners, a suspected vessel is sighted and approached. Using well-recognized procedures for approaching and "visiting" the vessel, the master of the vessel asks questions about the vessel's origin, nationality, cargo, and destination. If there is reasonable suspicion that the occupants of the vessel are trafficking drugs, JIATF–South's mission switches from detection and monitoring to supporting law enforcement. JIATF–South seamlessly turns tactical control of the U.S. Navy ship over to a law enforcement organization, usually a U.S. Coast Guard District. The U.S. Coast Guard, through their law enforcement detachment (LEDET) placed on Navy vessels, conducts the law enforcement action and determines the disposition of suspected traffickers and seized evidence. While the Navy Commander always retains command of his or her ship, the on-board Coast Guard officer takes control of ship operations. Once law enforcement at sea is complete, the suspected traffickers and evidence are secured onboard the Navy ship by the LEDET. Tactical control of ship operations returns to JIATF–South and the Navy ship resumes its detection and monitoring mission.

[1] Allen G. McKee, comments on draft study via email, March 4, 2011.

for JIATF–South to Congress or the President, but neither it nor the task force has authority to compel cooperation from any agency beyond the requirement to do detection and monitoring through JIATF–South in its area of responsibility. As one former deputy director noted, "Some people like to tout that we are a national Task Force . . . the [NICCP] is a great cover document, but JIATF–South still plays by DOD rules."[159] It could be added that it plays by everyone's rules since the only compliance it demands, others have freely agreed upon in advance.

An important manifestation of the organizational support provided to JIATF–South is the latitude that organizational representatives have to make decisions. Liaisons from partner agencies are empowered by their parent organizations to make decisions that commit their agencies to action. As one JIATF–South leader noted, "All my interagency partners are GS–15 and empowered to speak for their agency. We never spoke to Washington."[160] The authority delegated to interagency personnel assigned to JIATF–South is a function of multiple factors, including mutual trust and the cohesive culture built up over time. As JIATF–South's reputation for success grew, it found it could demand more from other organizations and their representatives. However, it first had to treat its partners with great respect, ensuring that liaisons are fully integrated into the command structure and serve in key leadership positions.[161] It treats liaisons from foreign nations similarly with the result that they too are able to speak for their governments.[162]

The resources, authority, and record of success enjoyed by JIATF–South generate "emotional energy,"[163] a less tangible form of team empowerment sometimes referred to by researchers as "psychological empowerment." It is the conviction among team members that they can individually and as a team accomplish their mission.[164] A former director recalled, "People have to feel an empowerment and it has to pulse through the command."[165] Once the conviction takes root that success is possible and the team members are empowered to act, initiative grows and takes on a life of its own. JIATF–South team members believed "We were empowered to make decisions and felt that the leadership believed in us and would back us."[166] One interviewee noted that the JIATF–South director received far more suggestions for how to improve operations than anywhere else he had been.[167] There was "a lot of freedom to do what you thought was right."[168]

In summary, JIATF–South's empowerment grew over time, initially with modest top-down efforts that reinforced the organization's legitimacy as a national priority. These authorities were used to work out cooperative agreements for resource sharing that were carefully negotiated to maximize voluntary participation. Before these resources and authorities were available, JIATF–South's predecessors were ineffective. Once leadership forged enduring and productive partnerships with law enforcement agencies, particularly through the partnership with Panama Express, productivity shot up and JIATF–South experienced a powerful upsurge in "psychological empowerment." JIATF–South personnel are convinced that they can accomplish their mission and can continually improve the organization's performance. JIATF–South leaders are quick to insist that they can never forget the essentially voluntary nature of their enterprise and the attendant requirements for "organizational diplomacy." However, they also are quick to use the organization's growing stature to negotiate more favorable partnerships, be more demanding about the quality of personnel assigned to the organization, and be more muscular in tactical decisionmaking. In this manner, JIATF–South leaders have made the most of their limited de jure authorities to cobble together a fragile but highly effective resource sharing team.

3. *Organizational support.* As evident from the discussion of empowerment, teams typically are not self-sufficient, but rather require some level of organizational support from the

broader enterprise. Indeed, teams usually fail due to external organizational factors rather than internal ones. Lack of consistent strategic direction, inconsistent functional goals, and shifting resources are recurring causes of team failure.[169] Teams rely on a network of organizational processes connecting them to other elements at multiple levels and to the resources necessary to accomplish their goals.[170] Team-based organizations provide such support as a matter of policy and design, but the national security system is not currently team-based. On the contrary, support for teams is granted grudgingly and frequently retracted even when promised or initially provided.

Although we have already reviewed national security system support for the JIATF–South team in the earlier discussion of its history and in the discussion of purpose and empowerment, it is worth briefly reviewing as a separate explanatory variable for JIATF–South's performance. The most important point is that in the case of JIATF–South and its precursor organizations, support from the national security system evolved greatly over time. Initially, executive and legislative support provided legitimacy and direction for interagency counternarcotics missions by declaring the war on drugs a national priority, but this was not enough to overcome the inertia of the lead agency system. JTF–4 was supported reluctantly by DOD, which had an abundance of assets but not the cross-functional skills needed to perform effectively. Later, JIATF–East was kept in the DOD chain of command but given a monopoly over the mission to detect and monitor drug shipments and top-down support for a process to recruit interagency contributions.

Today, JIATF–South enjoys routine if not highly directive support in Washington, both as a matter of policy and of its well established record of success. Several Washington-based institutions are important. As a national level counterdrug task force, it is supported by the Office of National Drug Control Policy, which works to protect the integrity of JIATF–South's mission and ensures continued interagency support.[171] The U.S. Interdiction Coordinator, appointed by the director of ONDCP, coordinates the activities of agencies involved in detection, monitoring, and drug interdiction and oversees resource allocation to JIATF–South.[172] The Interdiction Coordinator is also responsible for oversight, coordination, and promulgation of the NICCP, which determines the "overarching operational architecture for organizations involved in interdicting illicit drugs" and codifies policy and organization for counterdrug operations.[173] The NICCP empowers JIATF–South as the sole authority for detection and monitoring of trafficking within its expansive area of responsibility as well as making it the lead for intelligence fusion, sorting, and handing-off for interdiction. It also stipulates that agencies working with JIATF–South will give it tactical control of their assets for operations.[174] The Interdiction Committee assesses the collective interagency interdiction performance vis-à-vis national disruption

In collaboration with the U.S. Navy, JIATF–South tests the utility of the high speed, experimental vessel Stiletto in a 2009 exercise area near the South Florida coast

U.S. Southern Command Public Affairs (Jose Ruiz)

goals, and also drafts the NICCP. The Committee is chaired by the Coast Guard Commandant and composed of the heads of 16 Federal agencies that have drug control responsibilities and budgets, including CBP, Coast Guard, DEA, and recently JIATF–South. Together, the Interdiction Coordinator and Interdiction Committee monitor the planning cycle for allocating assets and try to ensure that adequate resources are given to JIATF–South and that its location and scheduling is appropriate.[175]

Support from ONDCP and the Interdiction Committee is useful but not sufficient to ensure success. The ONDCP is often referred to as "a big dog with no teeth" because it cannot force agencies to support their commitments to JIATF–South and must rely instead on suasion.[176] It does have authority to amend agencies' budgets, but "it's not in any one's best interests to fight over it." Like JIATF–South, ONDCP values good working relationships with other agencies and works to secure voluntary cooperation.[177] Similarly, the Interdiction Committee is commonly characterized by consensus decisionmaking, or "law enforcement by committee."[178]

Although JIATF–South is a national task force, it is also embedded in the USSOUTHCOM chain of command. The JIATF–South relationship with USSOUTHCOM is important and has evolved like its relationship with national institutions. The relationship has been rocky in years past. In the late 1990s, many in USSOUTHCOM focused on the fact that JIATF–South was a subordinate command and believed its mission was to support their command.[179] Since JIATF–South was also a national task force, and one willing to push the envelope with new approaches, some subordinate commanders in USSOUTHCOM thought it was "too big for its britches"— "cowboys" operating without proper supervision.[180] The confident JIATF–South rejoinder was, "Yes, but we were successful cowboys."[181]

For a long time there was a perception at JIATF–South that USSOUTHCOM had an unofficial policy of limiting the independence of JIATF–South at every opportunity.[182] According to some with connections in USSOUTHCOM, they "had it out for JIATF–South," thinking "we'll tell them what to do."[183] The USSOUTHCOM commander has always had authority over DOD elements of JIATF–South, but in 1999, the command also took over JIATF–South's budget and personnel functions, arguing there was no need in such a small headquarters for duplicating those functions. Some in JIATF–South, however, interpreted this move as USSOUTHCOM asserting its authority over the task force. USSOUTHCOM commanders are sometimes tempted to use task force assets for their own priorities, such as improving relationships with countries in Latin America.[184] For their part, JIATF–South leaders approached USSOUTHCOM with circumspection, reluctant to fight too hard for resources and priorities.[185]

Yet JIATF–South has also received important support from USSOUTHCOM on major issues affecting its performance. For example, in 2003 General James Hill, USA, weighed in heavily in favor of expanding the JIATF–South area of operations, which was strongly resisted by USPACOM. Other USSOUTHCOM commanders, notably Admiral James Stavridis,[186] were also enthusiastic supporters, and the relationship has proven to be a source of strength for JIATF–South. For example, law enforcement agents working with the task force are able to use the command's facilities for weapons and small unit training. On a day-to-day basis, USSOUTHCOM takes a hands-off approach to JIATF–South. Far removed from both USSOUTHCOM's headquarters and Washington, DC, it is easy for the largely self-sufficient and successful task force to manage its own affairs. The fact that JIATF–South is both a national task force and a subordinate command of USSOUTHCOM provides justification for why it cannot uniformly follow the wishes of any one organization, latitude that suits JIATF–South just fine.[187]

In addition to managing its relationships with higher authorities, JIATF–South also attaches great importance to forging lateral partnerships with other independent entities. It is sometimes referred to as "COCOM [combatant command] lite" because it has managed to secure the productive support of so many different organizations that it can effectively serve as something of a command center for the drug war.[188] These relationships are a preoccupation of

JIATF–South, which realizes that "its success is totally dependent on everyone else" and that it is "nothing without these other folks' assets."[189] Some directors spend up to half their tour at JIATF–South away from Key West, traveling either to Washington, DC, or to foreign capitals to drum up support for the organization. As one former director mused, "I don't want to say 'schmoozing' because that sounds wrong, but you had to spend a lot of time talking to Washington to ensure their support."[190] In addition, interagency support is reinforced by the thousands of visitors who visit each year and report back favorably on task force activities. JIATF–South handles this volume of visitors with only four people in its protocol office.[191] So many visitors are an encumbrance, but the command believes the effort pays off handsomely with widespread support from Washington and many other partnering organizations.[192]

An important part of reaching out to other agencies is convincing them that JIATF–South would not take credit for drug seizures. Getting recognition for intercepting drug shipments and successfully prosecuting traffickers helps promote individual careers but also justifies agency budgets. When partnering organizations know they will be given due credit for their efforts, they are more likely to cooperate.[193] In fact, one of the most commonly cited reasons for JIATF–South's success is that other organizations believe they get a great return on their investment. In exchange for intelligence, personnel, funding, aircraft, or other assets, they get credit for drug seizures or prosecutions, making partnering with JIATF–South a productive investment.

Conveniently, JIATF–South isn't in charge of adjudicating credit for drug busts, which is done by the Maritime Operational Threat Response (MOTR) committee in accordance with its protocols. While interagency members of the MOTR committee address all maritime threats and hazards, disposition of the vast majority of maritime drug interdiction cases falls to the Department of Justice, the Coast Guard, and the Department of State. Deciding who gets credit—particularly in terms of who gets to prosecute suspects—is very contentious, so this process spares JIATF–South from alienating any of its partners.[194] Still, the task force has to work hard to make sure it keeps a low profile and that credit is given to law enforcement agencies. Until recently, JIATF–South did not have a public affairs officer, and it still routinely avoids publicity. Its directors must repeatedly convince USSOUTHCOM not to trumpet its achievements since that would alienate law enforcement agencies.[195]

In short, it is not possible to be successful without outside support. JIATF–South required some modest degree of initial empowerment from Washington to leverage the support of other organizations, but then had to work hard to secure that support with a self-effacing approach that ensures other organizations get more out of the relationship than they put in. The departments and agencies that make up the U.S. national security system typically have strong cultures and incentives to protect their equities. They "want to collaborate but on their own terms."[196] Put differently, "organizations are not self sacrificial; they will support a collective effort when they get something out of it."[197] As a CBP representative noted, "JIATF–South helps us get our job done . . . it extends CBP's reach way offshore. CBP gets more than it puts in, otherwise we would not [participate]."[198] As one former JIATF–South leader noted, it is the perfect example of the aphorism that an amazing amount can get done "when you don't care who gets the credit."[199]

Team-level Variables

We consider team structure, decisionmaking, culture, and learning to be "team-level variables" because, unlike organizational-level variables, they are typically the factors most immediately under the control of the team and they help explain day-to-day team performance. Team-level variables are attributes and processes that are shaped by the team and determine how the team operates. They are often the most salient characteristics to the casual observer because they regulate day-to-day operations. These variables also represent leverage points a team can most easily change to improve performance.

4. *Structure (location, size, tenure, communications)*. Team structure refers to the "mechanics" of teams—design, collocation, and networks—that affect productivity. Research shows that effective teams are designed to tackle specific tasks, are small (typically fewer than 10 people), collocated, and have a strong internal and external communications framework. Designing the team to match its work is important. The JIATF–South team design evolved along with its operational concept. The end-to-end problem-solving approach that follows drugs from production through shipment, interdiction, and prosecution broadened JIATF–South's inherently cross-functional approach. It required more functional competencies and thus partnering organizations, and put more emphasis on diverse intelligence collection and fusion so that actionable intelligence drove operations. Like other military commands, JIATF–South uses functional departmentalization to organize its personnel based on the similarity of tasks they perform (intelligence, operations, etc.). As intelligence began to drive operations, JIATF–South redistributed its internal assets to better support intelligence fusion and its Intelligence Directorate grew as a result. Also, as better intelligence enabled more productive operations, and as more partners participated in operations, the JIATF–South operations and Logistics Directorates paid more attention to detailed task design in the form of standard operating procedures that would allow diverse organizations to cooperate fluidly at the tactical level.

JIATF–South is unique in having created an extensive set of detailed interagency and international standard operating procedures. Its compendium of best operational practices is now codified in a 600-page manual that is updated on almost a daily basis and translated into several languages. Its interagency and international partners use the manual routinely,[200] and newcomers must "leave their respective asset employment doctrine at the door."[201] The standard operating procedures are based on years of practice and experimentation, but also on careful negotiations that demonstrate respect for other organizational practices. For example, the phrase *tactical control* has only one definition in the standard operating procedures, and it applies to everyone. Potential force providers who find the common definitions or components of the operational framework unacceptable are turned away "with deep regret."[202] Nevertheless, JIATF–South makes every effort to take into account the parent organization's "policies, directives, rules of engagement and legal authorities and constraints."[203] Over the years, the range of agreement on how to conduct operations has grown, as has compliance, but differences remain that must be accommodated. For example, the U.S. Air Force generally refuses to fly below 10,000 feet, but the Navy routinely flies at much lower altitudes. With this knowledge in hand, JIATF–South can choose what assets to use for certain missions, or how best to combine the strengths of different force providers.[204]

The size of the leadership team is another important structural characteristic. Teams that are too large become unwieldy and tend not to function as a team, but if a team is too small, it will not be able to accomplish its missions.[205] The JIATF–South command team is usually limited to between twelve and sixteen members,[206] including the director, vice director, deputy director, senior liaisons, and the heads of the staff Directorates. As needed, law enforcement agents or foreign liaisons may join the command group during the decisionmaking process. After options are developed, important decisions that impact the entire command may be deliberated upon by up to 30 people, including representatives from all agencies at JIATF–South.[207] However, this process is focused more on building consensus for a yes or no decision than creative problem-solving, making size less of an issue than for other teams. In this regard, JIATF–South sacrifices efficiency for effectiveness.[208] Subordinate teams operate at the Directorate level as well. The Intelligence Directorate, which is composed of around 250 personnel, has a number of small teams that perform intelligence fusion. The Operations Directorate similarly puts together small teams for the watch floor.

Tenure is "a bone of contention."[209] In general, JIATF–South wants new members to stay long enough to reach higher performance levels.[210] Since it takes 9 to 24 months before leaders really know their jobs, depending on the tasks and individuals, short tours are counterproductive. Many personnel just reach full productivity by the time they have to leave.[211] Similarly, every time a new foreign liaison officer comes to JIATF–South, relations between that country and JIATF–South cool until the new liaison learns to understand and trust the task force.

Participating organizations want short stays for their personnel—even 6-month temporary tours of duty. DOD is the big offender, often rotating its personnel out after 12 or 18 months. Tenure was particularly problematic in JTF–4. As a military command, its personnel only served for 3 years or less, which meant the entire organization frequently turned over.[212] As JIATF–South's reputation has grown, it has been able to require longer tours for key personnel. It now refuses to accept personnel for less than a year. Even so, over half of the personnel turn over every 2 to 3 years. JIATF–South now balances the turnover of interagency personnel with a core of long-term civilians:

> *Within JIATF South, nearly a dozen personnel in senior positions have worked against illicit trafficking within a National Task Force construct for 20+ years. One in four has worked this problem set while assigned to JIATF South in excess of a decade. Slightly less than 50% of the entire command has been aboard JIATF South for six years or more. To put any six year time span in perspective: DOD assigned personnel would have cycled through 2–3 times, USCG personnel 3 times.*[213]

Permanent civilians bring needed continuity and institutional memory but can also have a downside. They can become resistant to change and thus less dynamic. A former intelligence director acknowledged that after spending 4 years there, "you become part of the problem."[214]

Team research literature is consistent on the importance of collocation for team productivity. With relatively rapid turnover built into the design of the JIATF–South leadership team, collocation takes on greater importance. Collocating members is standard team practice and has many benefits. One study showed steep drops in productivity if members were located on different floors or more than a 100-foot walk from other members. "Virtual collocation" through video-teleconferencing, Internet chat programs, and other communication networks can partially offset geographic dispersion.[215] JIATF–South takes advantage of both physical and virtual collocation. Its participants agree there is no real substitute for collocation given the collaboration requirements of its core activity set. For example, the intelligence fusion alone was an exceedingly complex task involving at least 22 databases. Some artificial intelligence techniques could be applied, but there is no substitute for physical proximity and personal interaction.[216]

In 2003, the Operations and Intelligence watch floors were merged. Ironically, damage from Hurricane Wilma in 2005 provided opportunities for even greater physical collocation. During repairs and rebuilding, JIATF–South merged its Intelligence and Operations Directorates by knocking down the wall that separated their offices[217] and eliminated individual cubicles in favor of more open spaces.[218]

Collocation benefits collaboration and is reinforced by JIATF–South's relative isolation from higher headquarters and Washington, DC, where interagency turf battles are widely perceived to be more intense because they more immediately involve higher-level officials, larger egos, organizational budgets, and broader policy issues (for example, the relative benefits of crop eradication, interdiction, and social rehabilitation, among others).[219] With JIATF–South personnel in close proximity and removed from senior executives in their parent organizations, it is easier to bond and focus on the mission. If JIATF–South were colocated with higher headquarters (for example, in Miami with USSOUTHCOM), it would find itself devoting a lot of time and effort to supporting that headquarters.[220]

Some activities are necessarily dispersed as well, however. To compensate, the task force uses state-of-the-art communications infrastructure and liaison officers.[221] This system allows "access to information, know-how, and experts, but it also provides an easy way for members to feed important information back to their peers so knowledge that comes into the team can be monitored." The communications are universally regarded as superb. A former director likened the command center to the bridge on *Star Trek* and recalled fondly, "it was eye watering."[222] A system of computer networks and online chat rooms link JIATF–South with its external network of intelligence sources and partner organizations.[223] JIATF–South is also connected to foreign nations by the Cooperating Nations Information Exchange System, which enables online chat rooms that can translate language in real time.[224] New technologies also make it possible to rapidly share situational awareness by allowing JIATF–South to disseminate a "common operating picture" to its allies. JIATF–South gets constant inputs from all of its assets and fuses them in order to generate a map of friendly forces and targets of interest that it can share with its partners, thus improving operational coordination.

In summary, much of the JIATF–South structure is optimized for networking, both internally and externally. The core enterprise is well structured to perform its core tasks, and its interagency and international partners give the team expandable capacity and enhanced capabilities. It can reach back into its partner agencies, and it is also tied to an extensive external framework of intelligence providers including Panama Express, the El Paso Intelligence Center, and the tactical analysis teams it sends to source countries. These relationships must be constantly nurtured. In the words of one former director, "It's 'missionary' work."[225] However, the proselytizing is easier as JIATF–South's reputation for effectiveness has grown. Even historically aloof countries like Mexico have been successfully wooed,[226] and Canada required no cajoling at all, but instead asked to join. Long gone are the days with JIATF–South's J5 networked with other potential partners simply for engagement's sake. JIATF–South continues to invite partners to join but is no longer shy about demanding that they contribute to the team in return.[227] Moreover, JIATF–South now has a network of former employees who have taken up residence elsewhere in the U.S. Government and partner nations but continue to be big task force supporters.[228]

5. *Decisionmaking.* Cross-functional teams bring together people with different backgrounds and worldviews. Managed well, the resultant clash of beliefs and ideas "fosters a deeper understanding of task issues and an exchange of ideas that facilitates problem-solving, decisionmaking, and the generation of ideas."[229] The challenge is to ensure that diverse views are encouraged, ultimately reconciled in a manner that leads to good decisions, and not allowed to hamper vigorous decision implementation after the decision is made. Encouraging and reconciling diverse viewpoints can be more time-consuming and require far more patience and diplomacy than one normally finds in homogenous hierarchical organizations.

JIATF–South certainly benefits from diverse viewpoints given the wide variety of organizations represented. The key requirement is to ensure the diverse views lead to "productive conflict" that improves decisionmaking. At both the command group level and the daily operations level, decisionmaking at JIATF–South is usually based on consensus. If a decision to take action would present a risk to another agency's assets or equities, it is avoided.[230] Although the director does have the authority to override objections, it is reserved as a last resort in order not to alienate partners.[231]

Strategic decisions are collaboratively made by a command team consisting of the director, vice director, deputy director, senior liaisons, and the heads of the J-staff, although particularly important decisions may require the input of a group of as many as 20 to 30 people including representatives from all agencies at JIATF–South.[232] The emphasis on consensus means decisionmaking is transparent (there are no backroom deals) and slower than a directive approach. However, building consensus is critical for keeping all the disparate organizations in the fight.[233] For general decisions affecting the entire organization, every attempt is made to ensure there are no dissenters. If circumstances demand that someone's objections be overruled, the director will make a decision, but only with a lot of explaining. Although complete consensus is not often possible, there is always the sense that dissenting views are heard and amply considered.[234] Directors strongly prefer to work with and through the other agencies' senior representatives within JIATF–South. On the rare occasions that a director felt compelled to go past any organization's representative to their superiors for assistance, they usually got what they asked for because of JIATF–South's reputation for effectiveness.[235]

Day-to-day operational plans are prepared jointly by the Intelligence and Operations Directorates and then presented to the command team for approval.[236] After surveying the available intelligence and assets, a plan for employing the assets to best effect is created. Operational plans require the consent of the command team as well as any law enforcement agents who are providing the intelligence for the operation. Case agents are intimately concerned with the outcome of operations involving human intelligence sources. If carrying out a mission entails the risk of "burning" a source, the organization providing the critical intelligence can veto the operation. Here the law enforcement culture prevails, and top priority is given to preserving information sources. A poorly conceived operation also might compromise a source, so the case agent's views on the operation are carefully considered as well.[237] In the end, the operations director makes a decision as judiciously as possible and always explains his rationale.[238] On rare occasions when there are differences of opinion about the risk involved in operations, appeals can be made to the director, who has ultimate authority to approve or dismiss the operation.[239] However, with good planning and communication between the Intelligence and Operations Directorates and the law enforcement liaisons, these conflicts are largely avoided.[240]

After the operational plans have been debated and approved, decisionmaking authority is transferred to the watch floor, which is staffed by both military and civilian personnel and handles the minute-by-minute direction of the operation. Here, decisionmaking is directive. The senior person on the watch floor, either military or civilian, can issue orders to the watch floor staff without asking for their consent.[241] If objections are raised during the operation, they are generally adjudicated by either the intelligence or operations director, although appeals can also be made directly to the director or his deputy.[242] At this level, the decisionmaking process is well established and requires little supervision.

The entire decisionmaking process is facilitated by a daily "battle rhythm" that sequences decisionmaking and makes its timing predictable on an hour-by-hour basis. There are meetings to share information and intelligence that accumulates overnight, administrative staff meetings, and lower-level planning meetings.[243] There are three separate intelligence briefings with varying levels of information depending on allied participation,[244] a classified briefing for the Americans involved, a less sensitive briefing for European partners, and a briefing in Spanish for Latin American partners. JIATF–South operates 24 hours a day in 8-hour shifts. Because at any given time one shift is on leave and another in training, the organization must support five working shifts.

Thus, decisionmaking at JIATF–South is time-consuming and gives greater priority to intelligence collection, fusion, and maintaining good relations with host nations than to

Go-fast boats are still used by drug traffickers, but the tactics for their employment are constantly changing

conducting operations.[245] Getting the support, or at least acquiescence, of the entire JIATF–South team also requires energy from the director and his leadership cadre. Leaders must often attend multiple briefings on the same operation. This is "cumbersome but necessary" as high levels of cooperation can only be sustained if everyone feels part of the decisionmaking process and all are being treated as full partners. Collaborative decisionmaking takes longer than an authoritative model, but produces better solutions and maintains the support of interagency and international partners.[246] Once basic plans are approved, however, the directive decisionmaking process on the watch floor is authoritative because real-time operations require rapid decisions that can't be contingent on consensus-building debate.

6. *Culture.* The standard definition of organizational culture as shared values, norms, and beliefs also applies to teams. Team culture, like all organizational culture, can be hard to identify and assess. One basic indicator of a strong culture is cohesion, which can be assessed by member commitment to the team's mission. JIATF–South personnel are well known for being passionate about their work.[247] Many view the JIATF–South mission as a "moral imperative" rather than just a job.[248] "Everyone dislikes drug traffickers," and many are so committed to the mission they stay on despite the high cost of living in Key West. The sense of urgency that comes with being responsible for real operations "in the middle of a war zone"[249] reinforces the sense of commitment. Many foreign liaison officers like being assigned to JIATF–South because they know their ability to directly engage real world threats will far exceed what they might otherwise do and learn in any other assignment back home.[250] Even those who are not directly involved in executing operations know they are making a difference: "If we didn't do something right [in the J4] they won't get the drug traffickers."[251] A widely shared sentiment, regardless of

one's role, was that "the best guys here spend a day at the war, not in the office."[252] Victories in the ongoing war are celebrated by hoisting a "cocaine flag" in front of the headquarters every time JIATF–South contributes to a drug bust.[253]

It takes time, however, to develop a positive team culture. Members must overcome their parochial Service, agency, or personal worldviews, appreciate diverse perspectives, and be committed to fulfilling the team purpose by working as an integrated unit.[254] But newcomers to JIATF–South usually experience culture shock, feeling "dazed and confused and scared."[255] Some confess that the complexity of the operations leaves them feeling they are moving too slowly or are overreacting when they do take action. Newcomers often have had little experience working with people outside their own Service or agency. After arriving, they are acutely aware that they have entered a different culture, surrounded by a bewildering array of unfamiliar uniforms and languages, or as the familiar quip goes, "the *Star Wars* bar scene."[256]

Civilians from outside DOD often find JIATF–South to be overwhelmingly military. A recently arrived DEA liaison recalled a conversation with such a blizzard of acronyms that he was unsure what had been said and was irritated by having to fill out multiple versions of paperwork just to get access to his new office.[257] On the other hand, DOD personnel are shocked at how casual and freewheeling JIATF–South is. Some are scandalized to hear law enforcement officials openly discuss sensitive subjects or readily circumvent standard operating procedures. One military pilot observed that "flying with Customs is like flying with your dad . . . everyone is over 50." The interagency cultural divide can be more difficult to bridge than international differences. At the social gatherings frequently held to build team unity, people commonly gather by functional background regardless of national origin and language proficiency.[258]

Over time, the clash of cultures has diminished. When the organization was overwhelmingly military, *civilian* was a curse word."[259] Those in uniform "would have felt more comfortable and familiar with the Russian fleet in Vladivostok than with . . . the DEA, who were more horizontal, didn't have an op[erational] plan or schedule, [and] were more comfortable blending in with the locals." Now the military has learned to appreciate the law enforcement culture, understanding that its members are as patriotic as the military, and that the best Federal agents are really good at what they do.[260] It also is common to hear civilians express appreciation for the military discipline that serves as a backbone for all JIATF–South activities.

Teams with high levels of trust are more likely to accomplish complex tasks,[261] and building trust was the singular requirement for bridging the culture gap at JIATF–South. As one source noted, building trust was not magic, just hard work. Trust is built and maintained in several ways at JIATF–South. It is helped along by socializing: "You need to go drinking with the DEA guys, schmooze with the ambassadors."[262] The same is true for building trust inside the team. As one agent noted, the camaraderie at JIATF–South is so strong it "seems more like a fraternity where you adapt to group norms."[263] Team members are encouraged to get away from the computer and "mix and mingle," because the more people you know, the more ways you can find to solve problems. Geography plays a role; because Key West "is in the middle of nowhere," people spend a lot of time together and are more willing to hang out after work because of the short commute.[264] JIATF–South is also unique in that most people are excited to be there,[265] and a great deal of effort is made to make newcomers feel welcome.[266] It is made clear to them from the very beginning that they are expected to work hard and work together. This peer pressure encourages people to work as a team.[267]

While socializing is vital, deep trust also requires shared experience. A CBP representative recalled that earlier in his career the Customs Service had not trusted either JIATF–South (in Panama) or JIATF–East. JIATF–South finally convinced Customs to send liaisons to sit in on the watch floor and help with targeting, but it took years of painful negotiations on standard operating procedures before Customs felt it could trust JIATF–South enough to relinquish tactical control of its assets. Even then, Customs "initially ignored the ones we did not like." Now, however, "we trust that our airplanes will be targeted properly and that they will respect our rules and regulations."[268]

Once trust is established, it must be maintained, and the JIATF–South culture is tailormade to support trust relationships. When asked to characterize the JIATF–South culture, the most frequently mentioned attributes—collaborative, open, transparent, information-sharing—are all conducive of trust. So are the second most frequently cited attributes: respect and politeness. Even during contentious debate, "we are very polite here."[269] For some civilian law enforcement members, the politeness initially seems like a military attribute. However, they come to understand they are being shown respect in order to establish a collaborative environment. Everyone is accorded respect, regardless of the contribution their organization makes to the collective enterprise.[270] In the long run, it pays off, since at some point that person and his or her organization will be able to make a critical contribution. Establishing trust through respect and politeness also requires bending some rules. For example, to establish trust, foreign liaisons are included in the command center when their countries are involved because it would be offensive and reduce their effectiveness to freeze them out and embarrass them.

One JIATF–South member responsible for training insisted on "the need to be ruthless about a couple of very important guidelines" that greatly facilitate trust:

- No single group has all the answers.

- Each agency has a set of organizational competencies that should be respected and leveraged.

- Each group has particular procedures that need to be respected and integrated.[271]

These mores stem from the fact that JIATF–South "provides military assistance to law enforcement,"[272] which requires a special relationship with the law enforcement organizations that are indispensable to the task force's performance (providing more than 80 percent of the actionable intelligence leading to drug disruptions). Trust is at the core of law enforcement culture. Unlike national security agencies, law enforcement agencies decentralize security, allowing their case agents to decide how to classify evidence and with whom to share it. Naturally enough, most law enforcement officials are wary of sharing their information with strangers. Even as recently as 2002, many interagency personnel did not share intelligence except by word of mouth with those they trusted. This tendency abated with the establishment of interagency communication systems[273] and years of assiduous work by JIATF–South to earn the trust of law enforcement agencies.

An important breakthrough came when JIATF–South partnered with Panama Express, a relationship based on a serendipitous personal connection. Just as Panama Express was getting under way, a new director came to JIATF–South. By coincidence, as a then young Coast Guard lieutenant, Rear Admiral David Belz lived next door to a captain in the Marine Corps who later became an FBI agent and the head of Panama Express. This history allowed them to quickly establish a trusting relationship. Panama Express shared intelligence with JIATF–South, and JIATF–South provided material support to Panama Express.[274] JIATF–South civilians help provide continuity for the trust relationships once they are established,[275] which is essential for the long-term success of the organization: "the core of this kind of thing is the continuity of trust."[276]

Trust is fragile. A CBP representative marveled at the "gigantic bubble of trust here" at JIATF–South, an apt metaphor suggesting how quickly trust can disappear. As one military member observed, "If you burn a law enforcement guy once, he'll never give you another chance."[277] The CBP officer agreed, noting "one mistake and it is gone." However, he also observed that trust is built over time and can be rebuilt after mistakes have been made. He noted there have been incidents that diminished trust yet the relationships were mended. But "if there are a couple of mistakes, it is a real setback." He also observed that since trust is based on relationships, it takes a hit when personnel rotate out or the organization changes location. When the old JIATF–South moved from Panama City and merged with JIATF–East in Key West, for example, it had to reestablish the relationship with Customs personnel. When trust diminishes, it is imperative that it be built back up. With so much work to do and so few people, it is "amazing that JIATF–South functions" so well, and it only works because trust has been built up.[278]

There are other less salient but still important aspects of the JIATF–South culture that support high performance. Individual empowerment is the norm. Leaders rely on subordinates to know answers rather than acting like they, as leaders, must know everything (unlike some military Service cultures, one interviewee noted). Individuals are also expected to "push the envelope without going to jail."[279] Team members overwhelmingly feel that their superiors trust them, support their taking initiative,[280] and encourage them to come up with experimental ideas to help the organization keep pace with the smugglers.[281] A former member observed, "I was never turned down on any proposal made to improve things, and ideas came from contractors and junior analysts too."[282] Some members of JIATF–South characterize this attribute more generally as a problem-solving culture an openness to learning[283] and trying new things. One member worried that after 19 years a bit of complacency is settling in, and a former leader noted that because JIATF–South is trusted and receives so little oversight, it is particularly important that it remain open to self-criticism and improvements.[284] If there is an incipient tendency for JIATF–South to "rest on its laurels," the best antidote is probably a culture where people continue to believe that they are empowered to act and that their contributions are valued, and all those we interviewed believe that is the case at JIATF–South.

7. *Learning.* For teams to remain effective in a dynamic environment, they must learn quickly and adapt. Drug traffickers have a well-deserved reputation for being clever and agile; just keeping up with them requires a great degree of organizational nimbleness. Colossal mistakes were made in the beginning. The attitude "was 'we'll crush the druggies' but instead we couldn't even find them."[285] The JIATF–South leaders first had to learn how to make the basic enterprise work. Most fundamentally, they had to learn to integrate intelligence and operations, and prioritize resources accordingly.

In JTF–4, the Operations Directorate had been the most important. Although JTF–4 was created as an intelligence fusion center, the Intelligence and Operations Directorates did not cooperate. Instead, most of the JTF–4 operations were based on the principle of "sailing around blindly."[286] This brute force method was relatively successful as long as the task force had access to plenty of ships and planes. Eventually, these resources dried up and austerity stimulated innovation, which led to a greater appreciation for intelligence fusion. By 2000, the power of intelligence to cue operations was appreciated and the Intelligence Directorate was absorbing a large portion of JIATF–South resources. The Intelligence Directorate eventually eclipsed the Operations and Planning Directorates and now makes up roughly half of JIATF–South's overall manpower.

More generally, JIATF–South leaders had to learn the goals and incentives that drove other agency behaviors. A perfect example of JIATF–South learning was its changing attitude towards arrests. The task force, as a primarily military organization, did not pay attention to prosecuting traffickers. That was not the DOD mission, neither was it something the military knew how to do, nor cared to learn. As an interagency organization, however, the increasing involvement of law enforcement agents required paying attention to arrests and prosecutions. Besides the fact that it simply makes sense to try to prosecute and imprison smugglers, some law enforcement agencies (particularly the DEA) prize people over drugs; improving its prosecution record consequently became more important to JIATF–South. This encouraged the law enforcement officers to collaborate with JIATF–South and provide it with intelligence, which led to more operations and thus improved its drug seizures and also led to more arrests, which led in turn to more prosecutions and more intelligence sources. It did not take long for DEA and the rest of the law enforcement community to see that their support to JIATF–South could lead to successful prosecutions that were in the interests of their respective organizations.

One outcome of this learning process has been that the entire enterprise, including its network of supporters, can influence the likelihood that traffickers will be prosecuted. Because the JIATF–South area of responsibility covers many legal jurisdictions, U.S. officials can influence where a suspected smuggler will be prosecuted by tracking him over a long swathe of ocean and then arresting him where there is a better chance that he will be given a stiff sentence. One preferred location is the Middle District of Florida, in Tampa. Although other jurisdictions have developed expertise in dealing with the novel issues that arise in these prosecutions,[287] smugglers are often brought to Tampa even if they have been caught in the Pacific. Many investigations are run from that district, which benefits from the presence of one of the Nation's top drug prosecutors and a well developed body of relevant case law. Accordingly, smugglers who face long jail terms will often agree to work for Panama Express (also located in that district) in order to receive lighter sentencing. This rewards both the law enforcement officials, who get credit for the arrest, and JIATF–South, which gets a new source of intelligence. Similarly, JIATF–South likes working with the French Navy (which has maritime law enforcement authorities) because the French legal system is notoriously harsh on drug smuggling.[288] Such successes encourage JIATF–South to prioritize prosecutions as much as drug seizures.[289]

JIATF–South has also learned how to work with the security proclivities of agencies and countries with very different standards and regulations for classifying information and has an aggressive policy of disseminating intelligence to those who are in a position to use it.[290] One study noted, "JIATF–S[outh] is unique in having established effective procedures for routinely and quickly converting classified intelligence and sensitive law enforcement information into a form that can be shared at an unclassified level under bilateral agreements with partner nations capable of taking responsive actions."[291] JIATF–South has all sorts of accommodations for American and foreign partners including different types of firewalls to block off people who don't have appropriate security clearances or who might be a security liability.[292] Because many partner nations do not have high levels of operational security, JIATF–South has created an open source but encrypted forum for communicating information to outsiders.[293] Sometimes security rules need to be "bent" to push intelligence to partners or allies overseas, but because JIATF–South collects so many different types of intelligence, it is possible to package the necessary information in a manner that satisfies security requirements.[294]

What JIATF–South learns it passes on informally, as more experienced members mentor newcomers, but also formally through training programs and standard operating procedures. JIATF–South is one of the relatively rare interagency entities that emphasizes new member training. Perhaps reflecting its military roots, it recognized the importance of training long ago and institutionalized it. The amount of training members receive varies depending on their jobs. Everyone goes through a week-long orientation when they arrive, but a lot of this time is taken up by paperwork. An optional 2-week indoctrination course is available, covering basic American and international legal concepts, geography, military assets, communication systems, JIATF–South organization, and the command's "who's who." This gives new team members just enough knowledge to grasp what JIATF–South does and how it is done, but it provides no practical training. This indoctrination is also available in a condensed executive course for those who cannot spend 2 weeks in the classroom. Beyond this, training is left to the Directorates. Some departments, like the Planning Directorate, send their newcomers to an additional 2-week course;[295] personnel going to tactical analysis teams take a 4-week course before being sent abroad. Contractors are expected to show up fully trained and are prohibited by regulations from receiving specialized training. They do, however, attend the orientation and may be instructed and certified to make sure they are on the same page as everyone else.[296]

The most comprehensive training is given by the Intelligence and Operations Directorates, which have been conducting formal training since October 1996.[297] After the initial orientation and indoctrination courses, personnel from the Directorates are given an extra 3-week indoctrination course before being separated for further training by their departments (this training is available to personnel from other departments as well).[298] Those in the

Operations Directorate will have at least 10 more days of training, during which time they are given computer and job-specific instruction. Those destined for the watch floor will go through another 8 to 10 weeks of formal training, followed by a 6-month mentoring period.[299]

While this is a comparatively robust training program, considering the complexity of the organization, it is surprising that many people at JIATF–South get little training. Members of the command team generally receive only the executive course, meaning they have just a few hours of preparation before tackling their new jobs. One experienced staff member explained that taking time off for training is "a luxury we can't afford." JIATF–South is such an operational, action-oriented organization that training is always shortchanged by operational demands. It tries to make do by recruiting people with previous experience working in interagency or joint positions or who are intuitively collaborative.[300] Interviewees also emphasized the importance of "on the job training."[301]

Even so, there is a steep learning curve. For new team members, it "feels like you are in slow motion and everything is speeding around you."[302] New members have to learn how other agencies think, what their strengths are and what equities they have to protect, and how they communicate. They then must learn the same information about all of the partner nations.[303] Because of this complexity, it takes at least a year for a hard-working and open-minded person to become an effective team member and "it takes 2 to 3 years to really get it down."[304] Beyond the technical competence required by JIATF–South jobs, there is the requirement to meld with the collaborative culture, which for some who never "get it" is an insurmountable obstacle.[305]

The demanding work environment at JIATF–South explains the growing emphasis on training that can accelerate the individual member learning process, and the demanding operational challenge of keeping pace with resource-rich and creative drug organizations explains the JIATF–South emphasis on learning and experimentation. Since the collaborative environment encourages teamwork within and across Directorates, innovations can be multidimensional, involving new technologies and methods. As noted in the previous discussion of resources, JIATF–South has the advantage of attracting a lot of research and development funds for robust experimentation with new technologies. Overall, however, learning enabled JIATF–South to weather periods of austerity in the 1990s and following 9/11 when assets were pulled away for higher priorities and still to improve performance.

Individual-level Variables

The individual-level variables (team composition, rewards, and leadership) account for the impact of individuals on team productivity. Typically, the leader is considered the most

An MH–60S Sea Hawk helicopter from the littoral combat ship USS *Freedom* hovers over the position of illicit drugs dumped overboard by the crew of a high-speed go-fast vessel. Sailors and Coast Guardsmen from *Freedom* and Colombian navy sailors in a patrol boat search the area beneath the helicopter

U.S. Navy (Ed Early)

important individual on a team, but the entire composition is important. The way individuals are brought into the team, their disparate knowledge and skills, and how they are encouraged to use them for the benefit of the group are all important factors in team productivity. The more diverse individuals are melded into a productive team, the less dependent the team is on the leader for productivity. That has been the pattern at JIATF–South, where a common comment is that "personalities matter, but they leave and the organization still works."[306]

8. *Composition.* The literature on cross-functional teams has identified a number of individual characteristics that are positively related to team performance: creativity,[307] adaptability,[308] agreeableness, extraversion, emotional stability, team conscientiousness, and openness to experience,[309] to name a few. Beyond these attributes, cross-functional teams by definition require diverse skill sets. A wry quip is that the perfect JIATF–South team member would be a Coast Guard Reservist ship-driver with aviation experience who in civilian life was a 20-year DEA agent, spoke several languages, and went to a military staff college.[310] Because individuals with such diverse skills and personality attributes are rare, JIATF–South must obtain the full range of skills it needs by recruiting a diverse group of members and ensuring the individuals work well together.

Some teams get to hand-pick their membership, but not JIATF–South. Each partner organization assigns personnel to the task force based on its own personnel considerations and priorities. Early on, JIATF–East was seen as a backwater and was occasionally used as a dumping ground for undesirables;[311] "a lot of the people who came down here shouldn't have."[312] For many other liaison officers, going to JIATF–East meant spending too much time away from headquarters and missing promotions.[313] These factors did not make coming to Key West an attractive career step. However, as JIATF–South's reputation improved, it became an increasingly desirable place to work, particularly as a "twilight tour" for officials about to retire. The organization thus obtained experienced individuals with good contact networks, and who also proved more dedicated to the mission than "polishing their careers."[314] A hard-charging big ego is not the optimum profile for teamwork. As one leader noted, such individuals wouldn't work out given the JIATF–South approach and culture. Or as another said, if your attitude is its "my way or the highway, you are definitely headed for the highway."[315] Many "twilight tour" personnel made great contributions to JIATF–South and even stayed on, rehired as civilian staff. Their agencies' loss was the task force's gain.

Today, however, JIATF–South is more likely to be considered an attractive stepping stone for careers in either law enforcement or interagency operations.[316] DOD recently reinstated its practice of giving a flag officer (instead of a colonel or captain) the deputy director position, affirming the increasing attractiveness of a JIATF–South posting,[317] and it is now more common for personnel in other agencies to face stiff competition for a tour. One interviewee noted that both his predecessors had been promoted while working at JIATF–South and that he had to compete with numerous applicants from his home agency to get his posting.[318]

JIATF–South also now receives higher ranking liaison officers from foreign partners (typically an O–5/O–6 rather than an O–3/O–4).[319] It also gets high quality foreign liaison officers who are being fast-tracked to higher ranks. Many of the liaison officers from partner nations return home to promotions and assignments of greater responsibility. For example, one former liaison to JIATF–South immediately went on to head the Brazilian intelligence service.[320] The Netherlands provides a flag officer to command a task group it gives to JIATF–South (Netherlands Forces Caribbean), and on occasion the French Navy has also put a flag level task unit at the task force's disposal.[321]

While JIATF–South cannot hand-pick preferred personnel, its growing reputation does allow it to exercise more influence over personnel assignments. For example, it can specify the skill sets it needs for various positions, and agencies will now try to send qualified people.[322] In any case, JIATF–South is a broad enough organization that "everybody comes here with some sort of applicable experience."[323] Moreover, JIATF–South now feels free to move personnel to other positions when that is a better match for the individual and for itself. Some organizations, such as the Coast Guard, are upset when that happens, but such flexibility is considered to be "one of our strengths here."[324] In fact, some observe that JIATF–South personnel tend to "gravitate towards a position commensurate with their skills and personality type."[325]

The senior person from each agency is in charge of fitting new people into JIATF–South, and this generally works well.[326] Once someone's "umbilical cord" to their home organization is cut, the task force culture tends to change them slowly, making them more collaborative.[327] However, on occasion a big ego or otherwise unproductive person has to be sent away.[328] The ability to fire the occasional "bad apple"[329] is another personnel privilege that grew along with JIATF–South's reputation and influence. Previously, the task force would just be stuck with uncooperative people, but now it can call up their home agency to have them reassigned.[330] Even so, it is usually easier to simply ostracize the person and hope peer pressure gradually inclines them to collaborate.[331] As one interviewee with many years of experience noted, "If you're a hard ass you are marginalized in a day."

In addition to personnel assigned from other agencies, JIATF–South also hires full-time civilians and contractors. As JIATF–South evolved, its leaders hired people with the skills needed for long-term organizational growth, such as a training expert. As a result, it is a mix of long-term and short-term personnel with diverse backgrounds and functions. The mix fluctuates, but it is roughly a third Active-duty military, a third civilians, and a third liaison officers and contractors.[332] However, the civilian component is heavily retired military, particular in the Logistics Directorate, and 50 percent or more in the Intelligence, Operations, and Planning Directorates. This helps as these civilian hires understand military culture, procedures, and mission focus.[333] These long-term civilian DOD employees also provide JIATF–South with stability[334] and institutional knowledge.

On the other hand, the rotating military and other agency personnel counterbalance the long-term civilian core, providing new ideas and periodic reassessments of how business is done.[335] The military ethos also helps maintain discipline and retain focus, and it prevents people from going native in the notoriously casual Key West environment. It also provides a military command and control philosophy that constitutes "a strong backbone that other organizations can plug into."[336] Over time, certain Directorates have evolved to take greater advantage of the long-term civilian continuity, and other Directorates have leaned more heavily on the advantages of rotating military personnel. The Personnel, Logistics, and Communications Directorates are considered civilianized by some, while the Intelligence, Operations, and Planning Directorates remain military domains.

In other words, as would be expected in a cross-functional organization, there are subcultural cleavages or fissures at JIATF–South. Occasionally, relations between the different functional groups are strained. For example, there often are tensions over the placement of incoming personnel, and between organizations (CBP and DEA) and between the JIATF directorates, notably the intelligence, operations, and planning staffs, which can only grow at the expense of one another. Early on, the Operations Directorate was king. Later, the Planning Directorate gained strength as it became better at working with foreign partners. Heated discussions between the two directorate leaders were not uncommon. By 2002, the Intelligence Directorate had grown to roughly the same level as the Operations and Planning Directorates, and now it is the most influential. When directorate leaders rotate out, other directorates may take a run at the new director's people and resources.

The attitudinal and functional diversity at JIATF–South is therefore a great organizational strength but also a management challenge. Leadership must ensure no one group dominates the others in a way that would undermine the larger sense of mission that unifies the JIATF–South enterprise. Careful attention to team composition is one way the task force maintains a balance among its subgroups and ensures the focus is on performance and not personalities. Rewards are another way.

9. *Rewards.* The need to reward teams and their individual members is well recognized. Individuals need to be rewarded for their responsibilities as team members, but teams should also receive joint awards.[337] The most basic reward for team performance should be career enhancement. As discussed above, JIATF–South is now perceived to be a more attractive career option, and JIATF–South has also made progress on reducing or eliminating other disincentives to service in Key West, including its high cost of living. For a long time Federal pay for Key West was based on the "other than" location category, which meant a 32 percent pay cut from Washington, DC. As late as 2000, JIATF–East was unable to fill 20 percent of its staff billets because of its "inability to attract an adequate number of skilled personnel necessary to fill the positions, the scarcity of housing, and the high cost of living for civilian personnel living in Key West."[338] To compensate, JIATF–South recently gained approval for some of its civilians, including some foreign liaisons, to rent on-base housing.[339] In fact, JIATF–South subsidizes some foreign liaisons who would not otherwise be able to afford living in Key West. In addition, team members are generally one or two steps above the pay grade they might be elsewhere for their particular jobs, partly due to the need for extra money to deal with the cost of living, but also because JIATF–South needs and can retain senior people who are familiar with the organization's work.[340]

Effective teams must not only attract top talent; they must also reward their members for the kind of high performance they need. Like most organizations, JIATF–South provides a range of individual recognition and monetary rewards for its members. In the late 1990s, after JIATF–South and East merged, only military personnel received rewards. Later, changes were made so civilians could receive performance bonuses. Until recently, however, civilians were given an automatic monetary bonus simply for working in Key West because the cost-of-living allowance for Federal employees was far too low. A systematic effort is also made by JIATF–South to give out nonmonetary rewards such as medals and plaques.[341] What really matters, however, is getting persons recognized and rewarded by their parent organizations. Depending on what agency team members come from, it is not always possible to obtain such commendations, but directorate heads try to make sure good team members leave with letters of recommendation for their home agencies.[342]

Unquestionably, the most important reward at JIATF–South is job satisfaction. The universal sentiment is that the work at JIATF–South is deeply satisfying, and the testimonials are effusive: "Best job I ever had,"[343] "Best tour I ever had,"[344] "The work was its own reward,"[345] "Best tour I had, great tour,"[346] "One of the most enjoyable positions I've held," and "An extraordinary experience; it was [the] most fun you could have." One interviewee mentioned he retired rather than return to his parent organization because the contrast in culture and performance was too disappointing. Another who did return to his organization noted he could no longer visit JIATF–South because it would only awaken remorse for the loss of the best work experience he ever had. Several factors explain the job satisfaction.

One commonly cited factor was "bottom up empowerment,"[347] or the "freedom to act."[348] It was not just empowerment, however, but the immediate feedback on performance from the operational environment: "You have freedom to take action *and* you see results."[349] One interviewee observed that the tight connection between performance and outcomes stands in stark contrast to most staff work at combatant commands where employees can't see their impact day to day.[350] Another noted it was "super energizing for junior analysts to see their work acted upon,"[351] not something that happens often in intelligence analysis positions. At their home agencies, analysts might spend months writing papers that only a few people ever read; seeing their work at JIATF–South lead to drug busts electrifies them.[352] "I work longer hours here than I ever had, but my job satisfaction is so much higher . . . [it's like] war without a whole lot of killing. [It's] something that has international significance. This makes it easy to put the 'A game' on."[353] Even those with a great deal of operational experience find this to be a very rewarding tour: "just like war and even more fun."[354]

The knowledge that each individual has an impact on the organization and is contributing to real world outcomes provides powerful positive reinforcement.[355] The impact of the near-term reinforcement[356] is magnified by the commitment to the mission. Most feel that the job is "a noble cause," a "noble mission." As one interviewee noted, "Everyone dislikes drug traffickers," who, as he pointed out, are the type of people who responded to JIATF–South's surge in effectiveness, which they did not understand, by simply "killing a lot of people."[357] Other interviewees noted that those on the JIATF–South team could be personally affected by drugs: "Drugs hurt all families," and "it gets personal fast."

In addition, and in part because of the noble mission of combating drug traffickers, there is a lot of peer pressure to perform well. As one longtime member remarked when asked about his motivation for high performance, "I just wanted to be respected." It is easier to earn respect in a high-performing organization like JIATF–South. The empowerment, immediate performance feedback, commitment to the mission, and culture all make for an unusually positive experience: "It was a very unique place; in 26 years of experience it was 'different.' All elements know they need each other."[358]

10. *Leadership.* Three different types of team leadership have been identified in organizational literature: external or formal leadership, in which the leader is a commanding figure responsible for the team and has authority over team members;[359] adaptive leadership or coaching,

in which the leader provides the team with guidance and resources and tries to remove obstacles that might block the team from performing to their highest capability;[360] and shared leadership, which distributes leadership roles and responsibilities throughout the team.[361] JIATF–South has experienced all three models of leadership. Between 1991 and 1996, JTF–4 and then JIATF–East was commanded by a Navy admiral, referred to as the task force commander. The Navy leadership style was very much the formal and directive model. Given that JTF–4 was a military command with a military culture and utilized hierarchical military chains of authority, the model was appropriate. Military personnel who had experience with the JTFs approved of this leadership style given the JTFs' lower levels of complexity.[362]

After JTF–4 became JIATF–East, the commander became a director. JIATF–East's director had to exercise greater tact in command and control of personnel from other departments and agencies.[363] The National Interdiction Command and Control Plan specifically limited the authority of the director in this regard, reassuring interagency partners that their personnel would not be "owned" by the JIATFs.[364] There is a consensus that the decision to fill the director's position with a Coast Guard flag officer was a wise one. Coast Guard officers are double-hatted as both military and law enforcement officials and are comfortable working with both military and civilian personnel. Due to the nature of their job, they also tend to have a more collaborative leadership style than military officers.[365] JIATF–East thus began gradually moving in the direction of adaptive leadership. The director provided direction for the team but devolved control of most activities to JIATF–East's directorates. If problems arose between team members, the director would intervene if necessary.[366]

For the past decade, JIATF–South has used a distributed, or shared, leadership model. The director typically determines strategic direction, performs ambassadorial work, and shields JIATF–South from unhelpful external interference. Externally, directors have to build partnerships with other agencies and countries and secure commitments from other organizations to provide assets in the coming year.[367] To do this effectively, they must understand the other organizational cultures and their incentive structures. Directors might spend half their time away from Key West trying to build relations with other agencies or countries, and are usually consumed by similar duties at home.[368] As a director, "you have to enjoy doing missionary work to get support."

Inside JIATF–South, parts of the team are routinely autonomous, and some directors have felt comfortable leaving the JIATF to run its internal affairs without day-to-day direction, choosing to concentrate instead on external affairs.[369] Delegating leadership responsibilities is not the same thing as abdicating leadership. In fact, directors had to engage the people they

Coast Guard Rear Admiral Joseph L. Nimmich assumes command of JIATF–South from Coast Guard Rear Admiral Jeffrey J. Hathaway, who led operations during 3 record-setting years of international cocaine seizures

were empowering even more intensively. One director's explanation of his approach aptly captures a shared leadership approach: "empower people, treat them right, listen to them, push them."[370] Directors have to make people feel needed and help them solve problems: "by rule, you take on everyone else's headaches."[371] One director recalls going home "mentally exhausted every day."[372] A director also described an experience akin to "herding cats. . . . I spent 90 percent of my time dealing with disenchanted team members. I sometimes missed the direct chain [of command]."[373]

A shared leadership model is appropriate given JIATF–South's adaptive enemy. Authority has to be pushed down to a low level so team members can make decisions rapidly without having to consult their superiors.[374] Personnel are free to independently communicate and work with partner nations as well as to speak on behalf of the admiral. Thus, directorate leaders have also adopted a shared leadership model, letting their departments run themselves while they focus on external affairs.[375] Similarly, the tactical analysis teams are empowered to plan operations with allies without having to consult Key West.[376] This is possible in part because they can rely on experienced long-term civilian staff members to handle routine matters, but more generally it reflects a culture that emphasizes trusting one's subordinates.[377] A former director recalled, "On the watch floor there'd be an O–3 and an E–6 moving ships and planes around, which would astound visitors. We would tell them that we don't have time to tell our watch officers what to do."[378]

Leading well in a distributed leadership model requires different skills, such as encouragement and listening. In the shared leadership model, the director must ensure that team members, as well as their parent agencies, always know their contribution is valued[379] and that they are empowered to take action. Active listening is also an important leadership skill in this model. Everyone, particularly individuals new to the command, needs to know his or her opinion is taken seriously. This means, for example, going out of one's way to call on people in meetings who aren't sharing, or sitting in on briefings for foreign officers even if one doesn't know the language.[380] Better yet, one director took it upon himself to learn Spanish so he could communicate better for the foreign liaisons.

Some people, particularly those used to military command relationships, are uncomfortable with this type of leadership and want a more formal style. They acknowledge that dealing with interagency partners requires a great deal of delicacy usually not found in formal/directive leaders.[381] They argue, however, that a more formal leadership style may sometimes be appropriate. For example, one interviewee thought JIATF–South directors could have been far more forceful in making the case for resources to USSOUTHCOM. He thought they lacked the gravitas of more traditional flag officers. On the other hand, for many people there is no turning back after learning and adapting to the JIATF–South culture and its shared leadership. One interviewee who moved on to another military command noted that he now cringes when he has to watch bombastic leaders who are incapable of listening. "Leaders who don't listen, who have all the answers . . . are not very attractive to watch. You have to be able to say, 'we need your help.'"[382] This is countercultural for the military, but essential if one wants to secure interagency cooperation.

To get JIATF–South on track required some traditional leadership that provided top-down direction, including the recognition that the organization needed a different leadership model and the willingness to institutionalize such change. Now that the organization is well established and operating successfully in the shared leadership mode, a more traditional hands-on leadership approach can do as much harm as good. A recent director with this leadership style alienated the team members and their parent agencies, leaving a tough job for his successor, who had to repair some damaged relations.[383] Reflecting on this experience, one JIATF–South member noted that in current circumstances, "arrogance is the unforgiveable sin." "The effective JIATF leader has to be able to deftly play the cards that he or she has been dealt, suffer fools, shield the command's members from higher level criticism, and allow others to take the credit while they take the blame."[384] It is a demanding, exhausting model of leadership that requires figuring out "how to get things done when you are not in charge."[385]

Maintaining Effectiveness: 2004 to Present

Before offering a net assessment of how the team performance variables collectively explain JIATF–South's performance, it is useful to summarize its performance over the last few years. In 2004, greater intelligence cueing capabilities meant that JIATF–South was able to monitor more than twice as many smuggling events as it had in 2000, even though it had fewer planes and ships. At the same time, hand-offs to law enforcement agencies improved. In the same year, JIATF–South was also able to disrupt 87 percent of all events it monitored in the western Caribbean and eastern Pacific, whereas in 2000 it disrupted only 59 percent of its monitored events in the same area.[386] Improving its organizational performance allowed it to double its annual cocaine disruptions during the same period.[387] Even though the enemy has proven elusive and adaptable, JIATF–South has maintained its record of success, and it has done so despite resource reductions. In 2003, JIATF–East could rely on the daily support of 20 U.S. and allied aircraft and 12 ships,[388] whereas by 2009 JIATF–South could expect only 4 long-range Maritime Patrol Aircraft, 4 airborne "use of force" assets, and 8 ships.[389] Even so, drug seizures in 2009 were more than 30 percent higher than in 2003.[390] By improving its intelligence, preparation, and coordination capabilities, JIATF–South has generated more interdictions and arrests over the decade.

JIATF–South's success is wholly dependent upon its interagency partnerships. Its intelligence-driven operations would not be possible without the human intelligence, authorities, and platforms contributed by civilian agencies, and it could not orchestrate all these contributions without the military organizational backbone contributed by DOD. As one former intelligence director noted, JIATF–South has unprecedented authority and control over all-source collection assets, both organic and nonorganic (national assets):

> We had wide ranging collection management authority, particularly in the imagery world but also with respect to SIGINT [signals intelligence] and the organic SIGINT resources which we controlled. As DEA and the [Panama Express/Organized Crime Drug Enforcement] Task Forces and allies provided us with more HUMINT [human intelligence] than we sometimes could handle, we would then use our imagery and SIGINT authorities to verify HUMINT source reporting and set up detection and monitoring traps and schemes.[391]

The ability to control and integrate diverse intelligence sources increases the impact of any given intelligence source, including human intelligence, and allows JIATF–South to use its scarce operational assets to best effect. For example, if a DEA agent finds out that a group of traffickers are using a particular means of electronic communication, the signals intelligence experts at JIATF–South can use this to pinpoint their location or intercept their communications by using electronic feeds coming from the El Paso Intelligence Center, collection points in South America, or from JIATF–South's organic signals intelligence.[392] Radar can then track the traffickers, allowing aircraft and ships to be cued to take up positions for interdiction.[393]

Because intelligence (human intelligence in particular) is the critical enabler, JIATF–South invests heavily in supporting law enforcement agencies. Approximately 10 percent of the JIATF staff serves on its 20 tactical analysis teams.[394] Not only does JIATF–South put some of its best people on the teams, but it also pays (along with USSOUTHCOM) for an extensive communications network across Latin America to support them.[395] Moreover, in exchange for DEA and State Department support for the tactical analysis teams, JIATF–South provides DOD counterdrug and related intelligence to Embassy Country Teams.[396] The task force supports its other major source of human intelligence, Panama Express, with funding, electronic information systems, and analysts; in return, Panama Express gives JIATF–South 30 percent of its cases.[397]

The work of JIATF–South is complex and in some respects more challenging than kinetic targeting. Working with law enforcement agencies requires a particular set of skills not normally found in DOD. Evidence must be assiduously gathered and detailed, criminal procedures must be followed, interrogations must be short, and leads must be pursued quickly. If suspects are successfully prosecuted, they may become informants and yield more intelligence for counterdrug operations.[398] JIATF–South must integrate the efforts of different organizations: agents and informants in South America, tactical analysis teams in Europe, law enforcement task forces in the United States, ships from the Navy and Coast Guard, planes from the Air Force and Customs, and Border Protection and diverse intelligence assets from numerous agencies, to name but a few of its allies. Like a funnel, JIATF–South draws people, information, money, and assets from many different sources and pours them on a problem.

Intelligence fusion alone is a daunting endeavor. Inside the Intelligence Directorate, 12 independent fusion cells analyze and fuse incoming intelligence. Working with the operations personnel on the watch floor, they create a "common operating picture" that shows targets being tracked throughout the operating area as well as where friendly forces are in real time. This information is then disseminated to all JIATF–South's force providers to help coordinate operations.[399] A former director gave Congress a sense of how complex the work is:

U.S. Customs and Border Protection

A semisubmersible craft is abandoned by its crew and sinks, releasing 11 bales of cocaine that bobbed to the surface

[O]ur most critical input comes from U.S. Law Enforcement. The information is fused with all-source intelligence, analyzed and sanitized as necessary, then aggressively disseminated to our tactical forces U.S. and our allies. . . . [t]he JOC [Joint Operating Center] *fuses multiple sources of radar, such as Relocatable Over-The-Horizon Radar (ROTHR), U.S. and allied ground based radars (GBR) located in both the source and transit zones and radar data from U.S. and allied ships and aircraft to form a single, fully integrated air picture. This radar picture is then exported to a great number of customers within the United States military and law enforcement agencies and as appropriate, to our allies.*[400]

Although the United States can perform detection and monitoring almost anywhere, American vessels may or may not be allowed to enter territorial waters, stop suspected trafficking vessels, or board and search them. Some foreign militaries, such as the French Navy, can perform law enforcement activities from which the U.S. military is legally barred.[401] Partnering with allied nations can increase the effectiveness of operations but also their level of difficulty. Working with and through partner nations requires using their laws and officials to arrest and prosecute smugglers,[402] so JIATF–South has developed a different set of agreements or understandings with

This vessel, its international crew—two Colombians, one Guatemalan, and one Sri Lankan—and its 4.1 tons of cocaine cargo were seized by U.S. Coast Guard cutter Sherman in November 2006, thus verifying rumors that narcotraffickers were using self-propelled semisubmersibles. It is now permanently berthed at JIATF–South headquarters in Key West, Florida.

JIATF–South (Allen G. McKee)

every country for how to handle interdictions and arrests. To communicate with allies during operations, JIATF–South has a secure proprietary chat room system (the Cooperating Nations Information Exchange System) that automatically translates conversations in real time.[403]

For its partners, JIATF–South is an unbeatable force multiplier that lets them accomplish things they could not achieve by themselves, and at a much lower cost. Law enforcement agencies "generate lots and lots of information . . . but what do you do with it? We don't run a navy."[404] Similarly, DOD can monitor but not arrest drug traffickers, and the Coast Guard can't accomplish its maritime interdiction mission without proper intelligence. Every agency knows that by collaborating together at JIATF–South they get a high return on investment. This is so much the case that CBP, for example, gives as much as 80 percent of its planes to JIATF–South because it knows they will be used effectively and that CBP will be given the credit for JIATF–South's successes.[405]

This collaborative, interagency record of success has been sustained against an intelligent, ruthless, well-funded, and adaptive foe. For example, the enemy targets JIATF–South just as it targets them. There is a constant threat of enemy penetration from drug traffickers as well as foreign intelligence. Drug traffickers have tried to infiltrate JIATF–South, and twice DOD employees were found to have been recruited by drug dealers (one was a junior officer who bought

With the assistance of DEA, Ecuador Anti-Narcotics Police Forces and military authorities seize a fully-operational submarine before its maiden voyage. Constructed in a remote jungle environment, it was seized in a tributary close to the Ecuador/Colombia border

an $800,000 house and a Mercedes immediately after coming to Key West). In response, JIATF–South must and does maintain a robust counterintelligence capability.[406]

In addition, traffickers are constantly adapting their tactics. They have taken to breaking drug shipments into smaller and more numerous loads to avoid losing too much in any one bust. They also send out empty ships as decoys. One recent tactic used by traffickers has been to have fishing vessels tow several go-fasts, of which only one or two will carry drugs. As soon as the smugglers come under surveillance, the go-fasts will race off in different directions with the hope that those carrying drugs will not be followed.[407] Such tactics have led to a decline in the ratio of events monitored to successful interdictions. In response, JIATF–South has had to increase the overall number of events it disrupts to maintain a steady level of cocaine disruptions.[408]

An even more troublesome change in traffickers' tactics and technology was the adaptation of semi- and fully submersible vessels. Rumors that drug cartels had developed a self-propelled, semisubmersible watercraft had been circulating since the mid-1990s, but it was hard to believe drug traffickers had their own submarine fleet. Some JIATF–South staff nicknamed the subs "Big Foot" because the rumored sightings could never be verified. However, dry-docked semisubmersibles were found in Colombia,[409] and finally in 2006 the U.S. Coast Guard, tipped off by JIATF–South, caught one in action (the prized trophy now sits outside the JIATF headquarters). Current estimates suggest traffickers may use as many as 120 semisubmersibles each year.[410] These single-use vessels can carry up to 10 tons of cocaine and travel as far as 2,000 miles.[411] Made of fiberglass and wood, they ride almost completely below the surface and are nearly impossible to detect. Recently, the DEA and Ecuadorian police found a fully submersible, 30-meter-long vessel, complete with conning tower, periscope, and air conditioning.[412] One estimate by the Department of Homeland Security suggests that over 30 percent of cocaine in the United States was transported by semisubmersibles.[413]

JIATF–South's success has also pushed traffickers further afield in search of new routes and destinations. Initially, traffickers could avoid the task force with an easy end run into the Eastern Pacific, but that option ended with the expansion of the JIATF–South area of operations in 2003. With the JIATF watching the Eastern Pacific, the drug cartels adopted new tactics. A picket line of fishing vessels carrying food and fuel 1,000 to 1,500 miles offshore was established first. Then huge, specially built go-fast boats with as many as eight engines would speed from fishing vessel to fishing vessel, trying to outrun JIATF–South. They would then come thousands of miles back to land, even just to reach Central America.[414] With the help of other countries, the task force is having success against these tactics as well.

The sustained effectiveness of JIATF–South has led to a gradual but apparently permanent migration in smuggling routes inwards toward Central America and out to the Atlantic. Drugs destined for the United States have increasingly been shipped in small vessels through the littoral areas of Central America.[415] Hiding close to land makes it easier for the smugglers to avoid detection. It also encumbers JIATF–South with having to make arrangements with local police forces to support interdiction. Once the drugs reach land, JIATF–South has to work through its tactical analysis teams and the DEA to support local police efforts.[416] Similarly, JIATF–South has forced smugglers to find new places to load and land their planes. In 2000, almost all the cocaine transported by air originated from landing strips in Colombia. The JIATF–South support to the Air-Bridge Denial Program, which gathers intelligence on air trafficking and coordinates the interdiction of airborne smuggling within Colombia, was so successful that by 2009 traffickers had almost completely stopped using Colombia. They made a wholesale shift to Venezuela, a relatively safe haven.

Some traffickers have decided to avoid the South-North shipping lanes altogether, reorienting themselves to supply drugs to Europe. Drugs from Peru and Ecuador transit Brazil where they are put on airplanes or ships bound for West Africa. There, shipments are transferred to vessels heading for the Iberian Peninsula. Once inside the European Union, there are no customs barriers to a shipment's diffusion.[417] As a result, European nations are increasingly interested in cooperating with JIATF–South to bolster their forward counternarcotics defenses. JIATF–South has

Two members of a law enforcement detachment survey the deck of the self-propelled, semisubmersible craft seized in September 2008 carrying seven tons of cocaine with an estimated street value of $187 million

U.S. Navy (Nico Figueroa)

reciprocated by putting tactical analysis teams in Western European embassies and embedding liaison officers in European counterdrug centers such as the Maritime Analysis and Operations Centre–Narcotics in Lisbon, Portugal.[418] JIATF–South is also interested in putting teams in West Africa[419] but so far has been rebuffed. There are also concerns that the cocaine trade may spread to the Middle East, where it might become a funding mechanism for terrorism.[420]

Counternarcotics effectiveness can be assessed in different ways, but JIATF–South is unquestionably a huge operational success. It covers an immense amount of territory with few operational platforms on patrol. The entire U.S. mainland can fit into just the Eastern Pacific region that JIATF–South must monitor, and at best the task force can afford to deploy only a handful of assets to that region, a situation analogous to patrolling the continental United States with only a few police patrol cars.[421] For this reason, the JIATF–South leadership team abandoned blind patrolling, adopted an intelligence-centric operating concept, and built an organization capable of sustained interagency collaboration. That success has allowed JIATF–South to stand toe-to-toe with the drug traffickers this past decade, driving up their costs, cutting their profits, raising their risk of prosecution and incarceration, and forcing them to divert their trade to less costly destinations. JIATF–South and its partners shield the U.S. population, protect U.S. rule of law institutions, and account for roughly 50 percent of global cocaine interdiction, and they have done it with fewer expensive platforms than they employed a decade ago.

Observations

The JIATF–South experience justifies several observations. First, the United States *can* do interagency, or whole-of-government, operations. Some skeptics believe that better interagency collaboration is as elusive as the Holy Grail or is simply not worth the effort, but JIATF–South serves notice that it is possible, effective, and, compared to the alternatives, efficient as well. The major improvements in JIATF–South's performance were a function of its organizational innovations, not the absolute amount of resources it was allocated. This truth points to the second major observation, which is that organization matters. The JIATF–South experience counters the popular Washington prejudice that good interagency collaboration is just a matter of picking talented and/or collaborative leaders. While good leadership in general and collaborative leadership in particular are highly desirable, JIATF–South's high performance has also required its attention to many other aspects of organizational performance.

Many observers who recognize JIATF–South's unusually high performance conclude that it must be explained by unique circumstances. However, we found that the factors they cite either are not unique to the JIATF or do not contribute greatly to performance. For example, some argue that the task force's success is personality driven and is thus not a useful model for other organizations.[422] The idea that organizational performance is personality driven is commonplace in Washington, and it is true that individual leaders matter. We found that the JIATF–South leadership made a major impact, particularly early in the development of the successful model that became JIATF–South. However, as noted in the discussion of leadership above, once well-established, the JIATF–South organization became much less dependent on any given leader. When the term "personality driven" is taken to mean that only key leaders who get along with each other matter, we have to disagree, because the evidence clearly indicates that other organizational performance variables matter more. It is also worth noting by way of prescription that the Nation cannot afford a national security system that is so fragile its performance depends on the rather unlikely identification of uniformly compatible personality types wherever collaboration is required.

Another common observation that implies JIATF–South's circumstances are unique is that it "is successful in part because it's a long way from Washington."[423] It is true that the distance from Washington facilitates team bonding and reduces some of the intensity of interagency disputes. However, other JIATFs (and interagency constructs) that are far removed do not work well at all, which suggests that JIATF–South's relative isolation is not a major explanatory factor in its success. Yet another observation is that the JIATF–South organization is unique in that it is structured with "unity of command."[424] As our analysis shows, it would be more accurate to say it achieves unity of effort without unified command.

A senior official in Washington spoke for many when he explained JIATF–South's success by noting that no one cares that much about drugs.[425] Higher priority national security issues would involve greater organizational equities and elicit greater organizational feuding. The history of JIATF–South, however, suggests the correlation between the importance of a mission and the willingness of autonomous organizations to cooperate is weak. Organizations involved in counterdrug activities had trouble cooperating before and after Washington declared drug trafficking a national security problem, and experience suggests the same could be said for other national security issues.

Others note that the JIATF–South operating area and focus on cocaine are unique. It is true that interdicting cocaine is a different challenge than stopping other drugs, for example the heroin and its precursor chemicals that JIATF–West must contend with. However, it is not clear that the JIATF–South interdiction task is notably easier. JIATF–South succeeds not because it is "shooting fish in a barrel," but because its interagency intelligence fusion pinpoints where the drugs are in the vast operating area it must cover. It monitors over 1,000 potential air and sea targets a day, looking for only 2 or 3 that it will zero in on as high priority suspects. Before JIATF–South perfected its organizational model, the drugs flowed so freely that pilots landing on Caribbean islands were openly greeted with cold beverages and paid entertainment.

Another critical operating factor often believed to be relatively unique to JIATF–South is that its interagency partners are compelled to collaborate by the uniquely rewarding operational environment. The argument is that they voluntarily participate but in reality have little alternative[426] since they get so much more out of the collaboration than they contribute. The presumption seems to be that only the unique flood of cocaine across the Caribbean offers such an opportunity for profitable collaboration. For example, skeptics point out in response to current efforts to replicate the JIATF–South model along the southwest border that local law enforcement has little incentive to work with Federal authorities, and certainly not DOD. Unlike the Caribbean, there is no need for a navy to interdict small boats, and local law enforcement authorities believe they control the best intelligence sources. It is true that collaboration works best when all parties benefit disproportionately, and that such might not be the case in all missions requiring interagency effort. However, there are several problems with the argument that collaboration requires a surefire super return on investment.

First, the need for voluntary cooperation—while true—should not be considered extraordinary. The current national security system has muscular functional organizations and weak interagency authorities, so virtually any interagency effort at collaboration requires voluntary support from the participating organizations. Yet the vast majority of voluntary interagency partnerships in the current system are ineffective because the semiautonomous national security organizations easily find ways to resist cooperation they do not like even when it is directed by the President. Thus the voluntary nature of interagency collaboration in the current system is a given and not a particularly helpful explanation for how JIATF–South found a way to make partnering agencies value their participation in its collective endeavor. Second, the voluntary participation due to disproportionate return on investment is to some extent an argument from effect to intent. It was not initially clear to the partners that they would get a lot more out of the collaboration than they put in. DOD, in particular, participated because it was directed to, and others took part on an experimental basis, which describes the breakthrough partnership with Panama Express. Finally, it is not clear that a target-rich environment is uniquely optimal for collaborative interagency ventures. Any problem that by its nature requires interagency collaboration for its solution and is sanctioned by national authorities would presumably earn laurels for participating organizations if they were credited for their contributions.

A better explanation for JIATF–South's exclusivity is that it benefits from 20 years of experimentation and gradual evolution. This assertion is an accurate historical observation, but not necessarily a good explanation for performance. Although it does take time for a leadership team and its larger organization to gel and become effective, it is not clear that it should take two decades to create an effective interagency organization. After the basic building blocks were in place by the end of the 1990s, and the leaders worked out how to partner with law enforcement, JIATF–South's performance took off relatively quickly. More to the point, if the factors that best explain JIATF–South's high performance can be understood, presumably they could be replicated elsewhere with fewer false starts and delays. Some of the performance variables examined—for example, culture—take time to develop, but not necessarily two decades. For most, there is no reason to think that the variables require a long period of gestation before becoming efficacious.

Certainly, mere longevity is no guarantee of success. For example, National Security Council interagency committees have been used for decades and their performance has been panned for just as long.[427] JIATF–West offers an even better comparison. It was created at the same time as JIATF–South and both were given similar missions,[428] but today they are very different organizations. Unlike JIATF–South, JIATF–West does not have tactical control over other agencies' ships and planes and focuses; it concentrates primarily on building the capacity of its partner nation's law enforcement agencies and collecting counterdrug intelligence, rather than directing interdictions.[429] The organization does not have a strong sense of purpose or a strong collaborative culture. The individual directorates do not collaborate well. The interagency partners are mostly interested in getting money from JIATF–West to support their own programs, and long-term employees "set up their own little kingdoms" to protect parochial interests.[430] These problems are compounded by the short tenure of JIATF–West directors, who tend to serve for less than 18 months (in 1 year there were four directors), giving them little time to make an impact on the command and inclining long-term employees to ignore them.

In short, we do not believe that the JIATF–South mission, environment, or other circumstances constitute a strong explanation for its performance. Organizational variables provide a much more compelling explanation for its steadily improving performance. Some close observers have noted the importance of unity of command (not quite correct), narrow mission focus, or the development of standard operating procedures that help partners interact.[431] All of these factors contribute to JIATF–South's success, but the 10 variables we examined provide a more comprehensive organizational explanation. They all contributed, and they all grew more efficacious over time as they interacted synergistically and were reinforced by JIATF–South's growing reputation. As the task force's performance improved, its sense of purpose was reinforced; psychological empowerment grew; partnering organizations contributed more willingly; the organization's physical configuration improved and its networks grew; its decisionmaking approach was refined and confidence in its efficacy grew; its collaborative culture grew stronger; it was easier to attract and reward members; and finally it became easier to delegate leadership as other parts of the model worked increasingly well. Success did breed more success.

That said, the history and analysis of JIATF–South indicate some variables were especially important and enabled the efficacy of other performance variables. To begin, the organizational-level variables seem to be the most important enablers. Both Congress and the executive branch indicated that countering the influx of drugs and drug-related violence was a major national priority, lending legitimacy to task force operations. JIATF–South translated this national declaration of purpose into a strong interagency sense of purpose that encapsulated an end-to-end concept for dealing with the problem. In doing that, JIATF–South leaders knew they had the support of national authorities even if they lacked the immediate support of their own organization or other participants.

Some degree of empowerment from national authorities also followed their declarations of purpose. In particular, the National Interdiction Command and Control Plan gave (then) JIATF–East both de jure authority and resources, stipulating that it was the only organization allowed to perform detection and monitoring within a large area. The plan encouraged the Coast Guard, DOD, and the Customs Service to expend resources through the JIATFs. The sense of purpose and empowerment also stimulated better organizational support for the JIATF team. Before these enablers were in place, the organization was not effective, nor was it very efficient, requiring far more platforms than JIATF–South can access today.

If national purpose and other organizational-level variables *enabled* JIATF–South's success, it still took a great deal of leadership to institute the team-level variables that made it actually happen. In particular, JIATF–South's early leadership teams had to structure the organization to support its end-to-end operational concept and then ensure decisionmaking was consistent with that mission and structure. It forged trust relationships with law enforcement and instituted a decisionmaking process that is countercultural for DOD. For example, without the refinement of appropriate decisionmaking processes that would build consensus among interagency partners yet allow enough flexibility and independence to carry out operations requiring split-second timing, JIATF–South would have either wallowed in indecision or alienated all its partners by abusing their confidence. The relationships and processes built by the leadership teams were fragile and had to be constantly nurtured, externally and internally. Fortunately, the task force benefited from a series of directors and talented leadership team members who, despite other differences in style, understood these imperatives.

Once these key elements were in place, other organizational performance variables could take effect. The JIATF–South unifying trust-based culture and emphasis on learning took root, and it was possible to attract more of the skill sets the organization needed. The balanced composition of long-term civilians and rotating interagency and military team members has allowed JIATF–South to reap the benefits of experience as well as encourage innovation. As these and the remaining performance elements were reinforced by success, the organization has learned how to institutionalize its success. Fortunately, most of the leaders coming on board recognized the need to migrate away from directive leadership to a team-based, distributed leadership model that empowers subordinates and gives experienced experts the freedom to deal with minute-by-minute problems in a dynamic task environment.

Collectively, the JIATF–South experience supports a final observation, which is that good interagency organization should not be left to chance. The national security system needs to understand how to create effective interagency teams. Even though JIATF–South receives wide-

Crew members from the United Kingdom's HMS *Iron Duke* successfully interdict a narcotics trafficking go-fast speedboat in the Caribbean in July 2009

UK MOD Crown © 2011

spread praise and more visitors than it cares to handle, its organizational innovations are not studied systematically, well understood, or respected outside of JIATF–South. This is regrettable. Other complex security problems also require interagency solutions, and studying the relatively few unqualified interagency successes that are available is a sensible starting point for lessons on how to improve interagency collaboration more generally.

While we believe JIATF–South is an important success story that deserves in-depth study, the model cannot be applied uncritically. The chances of emulating JIATF–South's success without a rigorous and holistic examination of its performance are not good. The Department of Homeland Security's July 2010 "Bottom-up Review Report" asserted that "DHS will unify the uses of technology, surveillance capabilities, and related resources across air, land, and maritime domains, with an increased emphasis on data collection, data processing, and integrating sensors across domains. DHS will harmonize operations and intelligence—utilizing concepts and structures modeled after JIATF–South."[432]

Nowhere, however, does the report indicate what it thinks the JIATF–South model actually is or why it works well. The practical limitation of reorganizing to facilitate interagency collaboration but without a deep understanding of all relevant performance variables may have been recently underscored by USSOUTHCOM's attempt to improve interagency collaboration through reorganization. While the changes worked in some respects, the command was unable to effectively perform its mission of providing relief to Haitian earthquake victims.[433]

Interestingly, one organization that did apparently take time to understand the JIATF–South experience was able to replicate its success. The U.S. Special Operations Command (US-SOCOM) benefited from the JIATF–South experience when putting together interagency high-value targeting teams in Iraq and Afghanistan. After 9/11, there was a great interest in learning how to improve intelligence collection and fusion. Both Secretary of Defense Donald Rumsfeld and Secretary of Homeland Security Tom Ridge saw JIATF–South (then JIATF–East) as an example the rest of the government could learn from and visited the command on several occasions.[434] After his initial visit in 2002, Rumsfeld was sufficiently impressed by the organization's targeting process that he told General Byran Brown, the commander of USSOCOM from 2003 to 2007, to get down to JIATF–South.[435] He also returned at least once more while Secretary of Defense, in 2005.[436] Brown did visit, and he invited JIATF–South to send representatives to USSOCOM to exchange information about technologies and techniques. Dell Dailey, the director of USSOCOM's Center for Special Operations, was also so impressed by JIATF–South that he visited the command every 3 months with his staff.[437] Another study conducted by the authors[438] concludes that the USSOCOM was able to emulate the JIATF–South key performance variables within a couple of years and that the results were a dramatic improvement in special operations performance.

Conclusion

We began our research assuming there would be a lot of analytic material on JIATF–South, particularly sponsored by national security organizations wanting to replicate its success. Instead, we found little work of this nature had been done.[439] Given the thousands of visitors that troop to JIATF–South each year to see how it operates, including many of the highest ranking officials in the national security system, one would expect otherwise. There are two likely explanations for the lack of interest. First, interagency research suffers from the "tragedy of the commons." Even though it is clearly in everyone's interest to better understand the relatively few interagency successes that the national security system has produced, it is not perceived to be in any given department's or agency's interest to conduct or fund such work.

Second, there is the widespread presumption examined above that JIATF–South is a unique organization that cannot be easily duplicated. Even many in JIATF–South, who best know the organization and its long history, believe it is a difficult model to replicate. Typically, they express hope that their pioneering work will indeed be the "wave of the future,"[440] but

Lessons from JIATF–South Experience

Although it is axiomatic that one cannot draw generalizations from a single case, the history and analysis of JIATF–South offered here does suggest that some performance variables were more important than others. It is worthwhile drawing out suppositions for further evaluation and substantiation in subsequent research. More immediately, some readers charged with facilitating or even leading their own interagency teams may wonder what practical lessons can be learned from the JIATF–South experience. We believe many merit immediate attention from practitioners:

Get a mandate from higher authority. The mission and the team must have sufficient legitimacy—that is, be clearly sanctioned by higher authority as a priority—in order to gain the cooperation of other organizations. Even if cooperation is on a voluntary basis, there should be a single organization dedicated to leading the effort. In the current system, you are not likely to be given directive authority over all the organizational activities that ultimately must be brought to bear on the problem. To overcome natural organizational tendencies to seek autonomy rather than collaboration, all parties involved must believe there are rewards for pursuing the mission. Both JTF–4 and JIATF–East/South had a sanctioned interagency mission, but the latter was also sanctioned by national authorities as the interagency organization to lead an interagency mission.

Tailor a holistic solution set to a discrete problem. It is easiest to forge collaboration around a discrete, clearly identifiable problem with a meaningful and measurable outcome. Using JIATF–South as an example, the mission is discrete and clearly identified (stopping drug trafficking from entering the United States); it requires cross-functionality (combining different types of intelligence, combining different assets from different Services, and securing the cooperation of international partners); and it results in a significant and identifiable outcome (drug shipments disrupted, traffickers prosecuted, drug cartels weakened). Take an end-to-end approach to conceptualizing the problem and the functional capabilities required for a solution to the problem, and then recruit the support required for the mission.

Know your partners. To build a coalition of partners willing to collaborate, the JIATF–South leadership had to learn about the other organizations it wanted to partner with, understand their equities, and appreciate what it would take to develop a trust relationship with them. These requirements in turn demanded a degree of open-mindedness, humility, patience, and persistence. Just like at JIATF–South, teams need to know how their mission ties into the missions of other organizations and have a broad understanding of the problem. This will help the team build networks, get support from other organizations, and attack the problem in a holistic manner.

Get resources. The national security system was not designed with teams in mind, and it will require extra work to make sure your team is adequately supported. This means getting top-down support in the form of resources and minimally sufficient levels of legal authority to use those resources with flexibility. Having an established resource base is particularly important as it will reduce the need to immediately barter with other organizations that may not be inclined to support the team effort. Resources also provide a powerful incentive for other organizations to partner with you. Over time, operational success and a willingness to share credit will likely attract additional resources from grateful partners. Finally, resources are a major indicator that national authorities take the mission seriously.

Build networks. Beyond the irreducible core of collaborating organizations that must be wooed, forging additional partnerships with varying levels of intensity is important. The complex problems national security teams tackle often require that they build networks with a diverse set of interested parties. This will help the team get better organizational support and allow it to draw from a wider pool of expertise and resources. These networks should be both horizontal and vertical: that is, the team needs to reach sideways to other independent but interested parties, but it should also reach up to higher authority that must be satisfied with the success of the enterprise, and down to subordinate or smaller entities that can deliver important peripheral but supporting capabilities.

Don'ts. Members of the JIATF–South leadership team also noted some common mistakes they believe others have made in standing up interagency teams of one sort or another. Among the top mistakes to avoid are:

- Don't command the presence of interagency personnel on your team.

- Don't segregate interagency staff in separate buildings.

- Don't disrespect smaller partners because they can make big contributions.

- Don't demand binding agreements on cooperation (at least initially).

- Don't ignore any partner's need to feel they make a contribution.

- Don't make binding decisions without substantial vetting and support.

- Don't forget to build a culture of trust and empowerment.

- Don't take the credit for collaborative success.

suspect it will be a long time in coming.[441] One analogy heard repeatedly is that JIATF–South did not have the advantage of top-down national legislation like DOD had when Congress passed the Goldwater-Nichols legislation mandating improvements in joint military operations. Therefore, it took JIATF–South two decades to put its reforms into effect; but on the other hand it also took DOD about the same amount of time to actually implement Goldwater-Nichols reforms. In other words, cross-organizational collaboration and culture change is difficult and time-consuming whether it is mandated top-down or built bottom-up. We suspect such successes can be engineered more quickly, as the example from special operations forces suggests, but acknowledge that a single case study provides insufficient justification for such optimism. Other organizations wanting to emulate JIATF–South's success need to proceed cautiously. In the sidebar "Lessons Learned," we offer some suggestions for how that might best be done.

What does seem quite clear is that JIATF–South deserves its accolade as the gold standard for interagency collaboration; it has proven its model and staying power as a high-performing interagency organization. It can be and often is argued that the implicit metric for JIATF–South's operational success—metric tons seized—is inferior to other measures of success such as profits seized or damage to the narcotrafficking organizations.[442] As we noted at the outset, however, our purpose here was not to evaluate counterdrug strategy or measures of success, but rather to examine how JIATF–South successfully forges interagency operations under the direction and guidelines it receives. Its ability to increase performance, defined by metric tons disrupted, and especially during periods of austerity when it had fewer interdiction assets at its disposal, is a particularly notable achievement—one that invites emulation in the currently constrained budget environment. More importantly, however, JIATF–South has demonstrated that interagency and multilateral collaboration is possible and efficacious precisely at a time when many national leaders are arguing that better interagency or whole-of-government solutions are essential for U.S. security. There is some interest on Capitol Hill in legislation to reform the national security system for better interagency performance.[443] The experience at JIATF–South suggests there are great benefits possible from institutionalizing interagency collaboration, but also indicates the need to proceed carefully with due attention to the variables that are critical prerequisites for high interagency performance. If national leaders do extract and institutionalize the appropriate lessons, then the remarkable JIATF–South experiment will pay off for the Nation in ways that extend far beyond the counterdrug mission it so successfully executes.

Notes

[1] The authors wish to express their appreciation to all the JIATF–South personnel who assisted with this research, and particularly to Allen G. McKee. Mr. McKee coordinated the visit to JIATF–South and unstintingly gave of his time to explain the intricacies of its history and operating experience, both during the visit and in subsequent phone conversations and emails.

[2] According to JIATF–South, "a JIATF–South disruption is defined by JIATF–South as a suspected narcotrafficking event where either intelligence and/or operational resources were consumed in the course of disrupting the event. Disruptions . . . are further defined as narcotrafficking events where the contraband was seized, jettisoned, or otherwise unrecoverable to the trafficker."

[3] Of that 40 metric tons, about half was seized at the border and another half was seized internally. Interview with Richard Booth, former vice director, JIATF–South, and current deputy executive director of the Interdiction Committee, December 13, 2010; Senate Armed Services Committee, Posture Statement of General Douglas M. Fraser, U.S. Southern Command, before the 111th Congress, March 11, 2010, 18.

[4] See James G. Stavridis, *Partnership for the Americas: Western Hemisphere Strategy and U.S. Southern Command* (Washington, DC: National Defense University Press, 2010), 82ff.

[5] *National Drug Control Strategy 2010*, 68, available at <http://www.whitehousedrugpolicy.gov/publications/policy/ndcs10/ndcs2010.pdf>.

[6] House Armed Services Committee, Posture Statement of Admiral James G. Stavridis, USN, Commander, U.S. Southern Command, before the 110th Congress, March 21, 2007, 21–22, available at <http://www.globalsecurity.org/military/library/congress/2007_hr/070321-stavridis.pdf>.

[7] The JIATF–South protocol office counts between 8,000 to 10,000 visitors a year, but many are there for conferences or other activities, not just for the express purpose of better understanding JIATF–South.

[8] House Committee on Transportation and Infrastructure, Subcommittee on Coast Guard and Maritime Transportation, testimony by Rear Admiral Wayne E. Justice, Assistant Commandant for Capabilities, *Overview of Coast Guard Drug and Migrant Interdiction*, March 11, 2009, available at <http://www.dhs.gov/ynews/testimony/testimony_1237405074399.shtm>.

[9] See, for example, Maria E. Bovill, "Redefining HHS International Response: Challenges and Recommendations for Interagency Partnerships," U.S. Army War College, August 2009, available at <http://www.dtic.mil/cgi-bin/GetTRDoc?AD=ADA510888&Location=U2&doc=GetTRDoc.pdf>; Derek S. Wessman, "Defense Support to Civil Authorities: Critical Capability or Vulnerability? Optimizing DOD's Domestic Range of Military Operations," Naval War College, May 2007, available at <http://www.dtic.mil/cgi-bin/GetTRDoc?AD=ADA470839&Location=U2&doc=GetTRDoc.pdf>.

[10] The authors would like to draw a distinction between JIATF–South's success in disrupting drug shipments and the overall success (or lack thereof) of the drug war. Interdiction is, and has been, a small fraction of the overall counterdrug effort, and it represents only one part of attempted supply-side reductions. Officials at JIATF–South and elsewhere in the U.S. Government acknowledge that tactical success at interdiction is unlikely to lead by itself to a significant decrease in the consumption of drugs in the United States. See, for example, *National Drug Control Strategy 2010*, 6; Hearing before the House

Subcommittee on Coast Guard and Maritime Transportation, Statement of Admiral Robert E. Kramek, USCG, U.S. Interdiction Coordinator, House Report 104-486, 104th Cong., 2[d] sess., August 1, 1995, available at <http://testimony.ost.dot.gov/test/pasttest/95test/Kramek3.pdf>, 5–6.

[11] Stephen Hadley and William Perry, "What Needs to Change to Defend America," *The Washington Post*, August 1, 2010, available at <http://www.washingtonpost.com/wp-dyn/content/article/2010/07/29/AR2010072905006.html?referrer=emailarticle>.

[12] For example, the Project on National Security Reform (PNSR) recommends placing a "hierarchy of decentralized teams" throughout the government to improve decisionmaking. See PNSR, *Forging a New Shield* (Arlington, VA: Center for the Study of the Presidency, 2008), 442–450. The Center for Strategic and International Studies "Beyond Goldwater-Nichols" report suggests using interagency teams to deal with complex contingencies. See Clark Murdock et al., "Beyond Goldwater-Nichols: U.S. Government and Defense Reform for a New Strategic Era," Phase 2 Report (Washington, DC: Center for Strategic and International Studies, July 2005), 20–21.

[13] See James Douglas Orton with Christopher J. Lamb, "Interagency National Security Teams: Can Social Science Contribute?" *PRISM* 2, no. 2 (Washington, DC: National Defense University Press, March 2011), 47–64.

[14] Fraser, 16; and Stavridis, 68.

[15] Stavridis, 68.

[16] Donald J. Mabry, "The U.S. Military and the War on Drugs," in *Drug Trafficking in the Americas*, ed. Bruce Bagley and William Walker (Miami: North-South Center Press, 1996), 43.

[17] "Coast Guard Law Enforcement Detachments (LEDETS): A History," available at <http://www.uscg.mil/History/articles/LEDET_History.asp>.

[18] Laurie Freeman and Jorge Luis Sierra, "Mexico: The Militarization Trap," in *Drugs and Democracy in Latin America: The Impact of U.S. Policy*, ed. Coletta Youngers and Eileen Rosin (Boulder: Lynne Rienner Publishers, 2005), 263.

[19] Drug Enforcement Administration History, available at <www.justice.gov/dea/history.htm>.

[20] Andrew Whitford and Jeff Yates, *Presidential Rhetoric and the Public Agenda: Constructing the War on Drugs* (Baltimore: Johns Hopkins University Press, 2009), 58.

[21] "Thirty Years of America's Drug War," PBS, available at <www.pbs.org/wgbh/pages/frontline/shows/drugs/cron/>.

[22] Interview with Anthony Placido, DEA, Chief of Intelligence and Assistant Administrator, August 30, 2010; interview with Admiral Dennis Sirois, Director of JIATF–East from 2002 to 2004, June 8, 2009.

[23] "DEA History Book, 1980–1985," available at <http://www.justice.gov/dea/pubs/history/1980-1985.html>.

[24] Placido; Sirois.

[25] Ronald Reagan, National Security Decision Directive 221, *Narcotics and National Security*, April 8, 1986, 3.

[26] *Anti-Drug Abuse Act of 1986*, HR 5484, PL 99–570, 99th Cong., available at <http://thomas.loc.gov/cgi-bin/bdquery/z?d099:HR05484:>.

[27] Robert L. Jackson, "Customs Service to Lead War on Drug Smugglers," *Los Angeles Times*,

May 31, 1987, available at <http://articles.latimes.com/1987-05-31/news/mn-9197_1>; see also Tony Payan, *Cops, Soldiers and Diplomats: Explaining Agency Behavior in the War on Drugs* (New York: Lexington Books, 2006), 49–52.

[28] Senate Committee on Foreign Relations, Subcommittee on Terrorism, Narcotics, and International Operations, *Drugs, Law Enforcement and Foreign Policy*, 100th Cong., 2d sess., December 1988, 1–3, in *Drugs in the Western Hemisphere*, ed. William Walker (Wilmington: Scholarly Resources, Inc., 1996).

[29] Raphael Perl, "U.S.-Andean Drug Policy," in *Drug Trafficking in the Americas*, ed. Bruce M. Bagley and William O. Walker (Miami: North-South Center Press, 1996), 31.

[30] *Anti-Drug Abuse Act of 1988*, HR 5210, 100th Cong., available at <http://thomas.loc.gov/cgi-bin/bdquery/z?d100:HR05210:@@@L&summ2=m&>.

[31] *National Defense Authorization Act, Fiscal Year 1989*, available at <http://thomas.loc.gov/cgi-bin/bdquery/R?d100:FLD002:@1(100+456)>.

[32] Richard Beardsworth, "Multilateral Narcotics Interdiction Measures in the Caribbean," in *The Political Economy of Drugs in the Caribbean*, ed. Ivelaw L. Griffith (New York: St. Martin's Press, 2000), 230.

[33] John Ahart and Gerald Stiles, "The Military's Entry into Air Interdiction of Drug Trafficking from South America" (Santa Monica: RAND, 1991), 27–28, available at <http://www.rand.org/pubs/notes/2007/N3275.pdf>.

[34] Daniel Lawner, Brandon Kaster, and Natalie Matthews, "Recipes for Failure and Keys to Success in Interagency Cooperation: Two Case Studies," *Defense Concepts* 4, no. 4, 26; Donald Miskill, Jr., "Command, Communications, Control and Intelligence: The Role of the Joint Task Force in the War on Drugs," Naval War College, May 14, 1990, 8, available at <http://www.dtic.mil/cgi-bin/GetTRDoc?AD=ADA323612&Location=U2&doc=GetTRDoc.pdf>.

[35] Payan, 113–115.

[36] House Committee on National Security, Veterans Affairs, and International Relations, testimony of the Assistant Deputy Director for Information Engineering, Defense Information Systems Agency, July 24, 2001, 10–13, available at <http://www.DOD.gov/DODgc/olc/docs/test01-07-24Deacy.rtf>.

[37] Miskill, 13–14.

[38] McKee, comments on draft study via email, January 24, 2011.

[39] Ibid., 14.

[40] Author interview with interviewee 7, July 9, 2010 (some interviews throughout were conducted in confidentiality; the names of these interviewees are withheld by mutual agreement); Miskill, 14–15.

[41] Ahart and Stiles, vi.

[42] McKee, comments.

[43] Ibid.

[44] Interviewee 7, July 7, 2010.

[45] Miskill, 9–11.

[46] Interview with Admiral Jeffrey Hathaway, Director of JIATF–South from 2004 to 2007, May

28, 2010.

[47] Hathaway, interview.

[48] Interview with Caryn Hollis, Principal Director, Counternarcotics and Global Threats for the Office of the Secretary of Defense, and former Partnering Director for USSOUTHCOM, August 18, 2010.

[49] Mabry, 44.

[50] Ahart and Stiles, 28.

[51] Based on a comparison of statistics found in the *Sourcebook of Criminal Justice Statistics* (2003), 390, available at <http://www.albany.edu/sourcebook/pdf/t436.pdf> and "JIATF–South Supported Disruptions," courtesy Allen G. McKee.

[52] Mitchell Locin, "U.S. Drug Policy Gets a New Look," *Chicago Tribune,* February 10, 1994; "NAFTA Can Help the War on Drugs," *The Washington Post,* August 22, 1993.

[53] William Walker, "The Foreign Narcotics Policy of the United States since 1980," in *Drugs in the Western Hemisphere,* ed. William Walker (Wilmington: Scholarly Resources, Inc., 1996), 230.

[54] House Committee on Government Reform and Oversight, *National Drug Policy: A Review of the Status of the Drug War,* March 19, 1996, available at <http://www.fas.org/irp/offdocs/pdd14_house.htm>.

[55] Angel Rabasa and Peter Chalk, *Colombian Labyrinth: The Synergy of Drugs and Insurgency and Its Implications for Regional Stability* (Santa Monica: RAND, 2001), 20.

[56] *National Drug Policy: A Review of the Status of the Drug War.*

[57] Ibid.

[58] We are indebted to Alan G. McKee for the point that ONDCP certifies and does not approve counterdrug budgets. PDD–14 provided that the Director of the Office of National Drug Control Policy (ONDCP) should appoint a Coordinator for Drug Interdiction "to ensure that assets dedicated by the Federal drug program agencies for interdiction are sufficient and that their use is properly integrated and optimized." PDD–14, November 3, 1993. See Drug Control: ONDCP Efforts to Manage the National Drug Control Budget: Report to the Chairman, Subcommittee on Criminal Justice, Drug Policy, and Human Resources, Committee on Government Reform, House of Representatives. Washington, DC: U.S. General Accounting Office, 1999.

[59] Executive Order 12880, November 16, 1993, available at <http://nodis3.gsfc.nasa.gov/displayEO.cfm?id=EO_12880_>.

[60] *Violent Crime Control and Law Enforcement Act of 1994,* HR 3355, Section 90201, "Implementation of National Drug Control Strategy," 103d Cong., 2d sess., available at <http://frwebgate.access.gpo.gov/cgi-bin/getdoc.cgi?dbname=103_cong_bills&docid=f:h3355enr.txt.pdf>.

[61] U.S. General Accounting Office (GAO), *Drug Control: Update on U.S. Interdiction Efforts in the Caribbean and Eastern Pacific,* Letter Report, October 15, 1997, available at <http://www.fas.org/irp/gao/nsiad98030.htm>.

[62] *National Drug Policy: A Review of the Status of the Drug War;* interviewee 16, a senior U.S. Government official with knowledge of counterdrug programs, August 18, 2010.

[63] Robert A. Remsing, "'Seams' of Inefficiency and Joint Interagency Task Force (JIATF) Operations," Naval War College, May 16, 2003, 4–5, available at <http://www.dtic.mil/cgi-bin/GetTRDoc?AD

=ADA420423&Location=U2&doc=GetTRDoc.pdf>.

[64] Office of National Drug Control, National Interdiction Command and Control Plan, May 1, 1999.

[65] McKee, comments.

[66] Interviewee 7, July 7, 2010.

[67] House Committee on Government Reform and Oversight, Hearing before the Subcommittee on National Security, International Affairs and Criminal Justice, *National Drug Control Policy: The Decline of Interdiction Efforts in the Caribbean*, 104th Cong., 2d sess., May 23, 1996, available at <http://www.access.gpo.gov/congress/house/pdf/104hrg/25185.pdf>.

[68] GAO, House Committee on Government Reform and Oversight, Subcommittee on National Security, International Affairs and Criminal Justice, Report to the Chairman, *Drug Control: U.S. Interdiction Efforts in the Caribbean Decline*, Letter Report, April 17, 1996, available at <http://www.druglibrary.org/Schaffer/govpubs/gao/gao52.htm>.

[69] Hathaway, interview.

[70] GAO, *Drug Control: Update on U.S. Interdiction Efforts in the Caribbean and Eastern Pacific*.

[71] Ibid.

[72] GAO, *Drug Control: U.S. Interdiction Efforts in the Caribbean Decline*, 2, 19–20.

[73] Ibid., 19–20.

[74] GAO, *Drug Control: Update on U.S. Interdiction Efforts in the Caribbean and Eastern Pacific*; GAO, *National Drug Control Policy: The Decline of Interdiction Efforts in the Caribbean*.

[75] GAO, *Drug Control: Update on U.S. Interdiction Efforts in the Caribbean and Eastern Pacific*.

[76] Interview with Greg Passic, Director of Drug Interdiction for CBP from 2004 to 2008 and Secretary of the Interdiction Committee from 2004 to 2006, June 11, 2010.

[77] GAO, *Drug Control: U.S. Interdiction Efforts in the Caribbean Decline*.

[78] GAO, *Drug Control: Update on U.S. Interdiction Efforts in the Caribbean and Eastern Pacific*.

[79] Interestingly, although JIATF–South was designated as a JIATF by the NICCP, it was not until March 16, 1998, that JIATF–South was given "a formally approved JIATF organization structure." Up until that point it had been used as part of the operations group at USSOUTHCOM.

[80] Interviewee 7, July 7, 2010.

[81] Interview with Deborah Angel-Schultz, a civilian in JIATF–South Logistics Directorate with previous military experience in JTF–4 and JIATF–East, July 8, 2010.

[82] Interview with Randy Ockman, JIATF–East Air Force Senior Liaison Officer in 2000, JIATF–East Director of Operations 2000 to 2002, and JIATF–East and South Deputy Director 2002 to 2004, June 30, 2010.

[83] John Cope, Center for Strategic Research Senior Fellow, email dated November 24, 2010, 12:25 p.m.; National Drug Control Strategy 2000, available at <http://www.ncjrs.gov/ondcppubs/publications/policy/ndcs00/chap3_5.html>.

[84] *National Drug Policy: A Review of the Status of the Drug War*.

[85] GAO, letter to Charles E. Grassley, *Drug Control: U.S. Efforts in Latin America and the Caribbean*, February 18, 2000, 8, available at <http://www.legistorm.com/showFile/L2xzX3Njb3JlL2dhby9wZGYvMjAwMC8y/ful30738.pdf>.

[86] GAO, *National Drug Control Policy: The Decline of Interdiction Efforts in the Caribbean*, 62.

[87] House Committee on Government Reform and Oversight, Hearing before the Subcommittee on National Security, International Affairs and Criminal Justice, *Coast Guard Interdiction Efforts in the Transit Zone*, 105th Cong., 1st sess., March 10, 1997, 31, available at <http://ftp.resource.org/gpo.gov/hearings/105h/41842.pdf>.

[88] GAO, Drug *Control: An Overview of U.S. Counterdrug Intelligence Activities*, June 1998, 40, 44, available at <http://www.au.af.mil/au/awc/awcgate/gao/ns98142.pdf>.

[89] Ibid., 48.

[90] Ibid., 48–51.

[91] Carrie Weimar, "Drug Trial Could Shake Colombia," *St. Petersburg Times*, July 9, 2009, available at <http://www.sptimes.com/2006/07/09/Tampabay/Drug_trial_could_shak.shtml>.

[92] Interview with Captain Marc Luoma, USN (Ret.), J2 from May 2003 to June 2007, June 15, 2010.

[93] Interviewee 15.

[94] Luoma, interview.

[95] McKee, comments.

[96] GAO, *Drug Control: An Overview of U.S. Counterdrug Intelligence Activities*.

[97] Marc Luoma, addendum to IDA Paper for Admiral Stavridis, 2.

[98] Luoma, interview.

[99] GAO, *Drug Control: Agencies Need to Plan for Likely Declines in Drug Interdiction Assets, and Develop Better Performance Measures for Transit Zone Operations*, November 2005, 4.

[100] Interviewee 16; interviewee 19.

[101] Interviewee 15.

[102] Sirois; Interviewee 15.

[103] Interviewee 15.

[104] Interviewee 5; interviewee 15; interviewee 19.

[105] Hathaway, interview.

[106] Interviewee 15.

[107] Stan Riveles, "Can Inter-Agency Organizations Succeed? A Review of the JIATF–South Experience," for official use only (FOUO), Institute for Defense Analyses.

[108] Sirois; interviewee 13.

[109] Hathaway, interview.

[110] Remsing, 14–15.

[111] Hathaway, interview. They operating areas were revised in the National Interdiction Command and Control Plan, which is discussed below.

[112] "Transit Zone Interdiction Operations, ONDCP Fact Sheet," Office of National Drug Control Policy, June 2006.

[113] Sirois; General Hill directed the name change on March 31, 2003, to be "effective as soon as practicable;" interview with Deborah Angel-Schultz, July 8, 2010.

[114] Orton and Lamb.

[108] John R. Katzenbach and Douglas K. Smith, *The Wisdom of Teams* (Boston: Harvard Busi-

ness School Press, 1993).

[109] Glenn H. Varney, "Control and Autonomy: The Primary Determinant of Successful Application for Self-Managing Work Teams," in *Advances in Interdisciplinary Studies of Work Teams*, Vol. 1, ed. Michael B. Beyerlein and Douglas A. Johnson (Greenwich, CT: JAI Press, 1994).

[110] Bradley L. Kirkman and Benson Rosen, "Antecedents and Consequences of Team Empowerment," *The Academy of Management Journal* 42, no. 1 (February 1999), 58–74.

[111] M.A. Campion, G.J. Medsker, and A.C. Higgs, "Relations between Work Group Characteristics and Effectiveness: Implications for Designing Effective Work Groups," *Personnel Psychology* 46 (1993), 823–850; Campion, E.M. Papper, and Medsker, "Relations between Work Team Characteristics and Effectiveness: A Replication and Extension," *Personnel Psychology* 49 (1996), 429–452.

[112] R.A. Guzzo, E. Salas, and Associates, eds., *Team Effectiveness and Decision Making in Organizations* (San Francisco: Jossey-Bass, 1995), 204–261.

[113] L. Argote, D. Gruenfeld, and C. Naquin, "Group Learning in Organizations," in *Groups at Work: Advances in Theory and Research*, ed. M.E. Turner (New York: Lawrence Erlbaum, 1999); see also "Multinational Organization Context: Implications for Team Learning and Performance," *Academy of Management Journal* 49 (2006), 501–518.

[114] Greg L. Stewart, "A Meta-Analytic Review of Relationships between Team Design Features and Team Performance," *Journal of Management* 32 (2006), 29–54.

[115] L.R. Gomez-Mejia and D.B. Balkin, "Effectiveness of Individual and Aggregate Compensation Strategies," *Industrial Relations* 28, no. 3 (1989), 431–445; Gomez-Mejia and Balkin, *Compensation, Organizational Strategy, and Firm Performance* (Cincinnati: South-Western Publishing, 1992).

[116] S.J. Zaccaro, A.L. Rittman, and M.A. Marks, "Team Leadership," *Leadership Quarterly* 12 (2001), 451–483.

[115] Campion, Medsker, and Higgs, 823–850; Campion, Papper, and Medsker, 429–452.

[116] Katzenbach and Smith, 49–50.

[117] House Committee on Government Reform, Subcommittee on Criminal Justice, Drug Policy, and Human Resources, *Interrupting Narco-Terrorist Threats on the High Seas: Do We Have Enough Wind in our Sails?* Statement of Rear Admiral Jeffrey Hathaway, Director, JIATF–South, 109th Cong., 1st sess., June 29, 2005, available at <http://www.access.gpo.gov/congress/house/pdf/109hrg/24892.pdf>.

[118] Angel-Schultz; interviewee 13.

[119] Luoma, interview.

[120] Interviewee 5.

[121] Interviewee 10; Richard Yeatman, "JIATF–South: Blueprint for Success," *Joint Force Quarterly* 42 (Fall 2006), available at <http://www.dtic.mil/doctrine/jel/jfq_pubs/4212.pdf>; Angel-Schultz; interviewee 13.

[122] Hathaway, interview.

[123] Interviewee 7, July 7–8, 2010.

[124] Interviewee 12.

[125] Luoma, interview.

[126] Passic.

[127] One JIATF–South director was told in his first meeting with ONDCP, "Cocaine is the priority."

[128] Interview with Mark Hollensen, Deputy Chief Patrol Agent, Miami [Florida] Border Patrol Sec-

tor. He noted JIATF–South could do more than it does, but retains a focus on the mission that is best funded.

[129] One former military member mentioned he had served with units that had a similarly strong sense of purpose; otherwise, interviewees agreed the tightly focused mission purpose was unique in their experience.

[130] Susan Albers Mohrman, Susan G. Cohen, and Allan M. Mohrman, Jr., *Designing Team-Based Organizations: New Forms for Knowledge Work* (San Francisco: Jossey-Bass Publishers, 1995), 275–279.

[131] Mark Matthews, "NASA Chief: Out 'Ultimate' Ambition is Mars," *Orlando Sentinel,* February 24, 2010, available at <http://articles.orlandosentinel.com/2010-02-24/news/os-nasa-administrator-testifies-20100224_1_constellation-program-michoud-assembly-facility-nasa-s-constellation>.

[132] Sirois; Luoma, interview; Ockman.

[133] Interviewee 19; Hollis.

[134] Interviewee 16; Ockman.

[135] For limitations on the types of support the Department of Defense (DOD) can give, see Public Law 101-510, Section 1004, "Additional Support for Counter-drug Activities," *National Defense Authorization Act*, 1991.

[136] Sirois; National Interdiction Command and Control Plan, May 1, 1999.

[137] Interviewee 7, July 9, 2010; Hathaway, statement, June 29, 2005; Passic.

[138] Interviewee 16; interviewee 19.

[139] The JCS publishes an annual counterdrug execute order that directs DOD support in accordance with DOD Global Force Management policy. The execute order "requests" support from Customs and Border Protection and the U.S. Coast Guard. See Angel-Schultz.

[140] Hathaway, interview.

[141] Interview with Sandy Brooks, Deputy J2 and Chief of Innovations and Technology at JIATF–South, and Special Advisor to the DCNO for Information Dominance Navy DISL, June 16, 2010; Sirois.

[142] Hathaway, interview; Passic.

[143] Luoma, interview.

[144] Brooks; interview with Sirois and email to authors, November 15, 2010.

[145] Sirois; interviewee 5.

[146] Interviewee 19.

[147] Committee on Experimentation and Rapid Prototyping in Support of Counterterrorism, *Experimentation and Rapid Prototyping in Support of Counterterrorism* (Washington, DC: National Academies Press, 2009), 20.

[148] Brooks; Sirois.

[149] Luoma, interview.

[150] Interviewee 5.

[151] Interviewee 16; Hollis.

[152] "Further, the committee reminds the Department that joint task forces of the Department that provide support to law enforcement agencies conducting counterdrug activities may provide similar support to law enforcement agencies conducting counterterrorism activities on the condition that

any support provided under this section is consistent with all applicable laws and regulations; that the support may only be provided in the geographic area of responsibility of the joint task force; and that a verifiable nexus exists between the individuals involved in the illegal narcotics trade and individuals involved in terrorist-related activities." Senate Report 111-035, *National Defense Authorization Act for Fiscal Year 2010*, 111th Cong., available at <http://thomas.loc.gov/cgi-bin/cpquery/?&sid=cp111pqt3&refer=&r_n=sr035.111&db_id=111&item=&sel=TOC_617117&>.

[153] "National Interdiction Command and Control Plan," effective March 17, 2010.

[154] Interviewee 16.

[155] Interviewee 7, July 7, 2010. The Intelligence Community has Title 50 authorities; the DEA and FBI have Title 3; the DEA, FBI, and ICE have Title 21; CBP and ICE have both Title 19 and 8; the Coast Guard has Title 14; the National Guard has Title 32 and 10; and DOD has Title 10 authorities.

[156] Hathaway, interview.

[157] Interviewee 19; follow-up clarification by email.

[158] Interviewee 5.

[159] Ockman.

[160] Sirois.

[161] Yeatman.

[162] Ockman.

[163] Katzenbach and Smith, 55.

[164] D.E. Hyatt and T.M. Ruddy, "An Examination of the Relationship between Work Group Characteristics and Performance: Once More into the Breech," *Personnel Psychology* 50 (1997), 553–585.

[165] Hathaway, interview.

[166] Ockman.

[167] Sirois.

[168] Interviewee 5.

[169] Mohrman, 82–83.

[170] "Why Some Teams Succeed (and So Many Don't)" in *Teams That Click*, ed. Loren Gary, et al. (Boston: Harvard Business School Publishing Corporation, 2004), 44.

[171] Riveles, 8.

[172] National Interdiction Command and Control Plan, August 31, 2005.

[173] Hollis.

[174] Interviewee 16.

[175] Ibid.; Kramek, 2.

[176] Hollis.

[177] Interviewee 19.

[178] Passic; Hathaway, interview.

[179] Sirois.

[180] Interviewee 7, July 7–8, 2010; Luoma, interview.

[181] Luoma, interview.

[182] Ibid.

[183] Ockman.

[184] Interviewee 7, July 7, 2010.

[185] Interviewee 5.

[186] See Stavridis, *Partnership for the Americas*, 82ff.

[187] Luoma, interview.

[188] Interviewee 10.

[189] Interviewee 15.

[190] Interviewee 15.

[191] Sirois.

[192] Interviewee 5.

[193] Sirois; Ockman; interviewee 5.

[194] Interviewee 19.

[195] Hathaway, interview.

[196] Interviewee 13.

[197] Interviewee 7, July 7–8, 2010. For example, it took years to get a representative from one unidentified intelligence agency, and it only happened then because that organization thought it would benefit from the posting.

[198] Interviewee 13.

[199] Ockman.

[200] Interviewee 7, July 9, 2010.

[201] Hathaway, statement, June 29, 2005.

[202] McKee, comments.

[203] National Interdiction Command and Control Plan, effective March 17, 2010.

[204] Interviewee 13; interviewee 12.

[205] Katzenbach and Smith, 45–47.

[206] Sirois.

[207] Hathaway, interview.

[208] Interviewee 7, July 7–8, 2010.

[209] Hathaway, interview.

[210] Robert D. Pritchard and Margaret D. Watson, "Understanding and Measuring Group Productivity," in *Group Process and Productivity* (Newbury Park, CA: Sage, 1991), 251–275.

[211] Ockman.

[212] Interviewee 7, July 8, 2010.

[213] McKee, comments.

[214] Luoma, interview.

[215] L.L. Martins, L.L. Gilson, and M.T. Maynard, "Virtual Teams: What Do We Know and Where Do We Go from Here?" *Journal of Management* 30 (2004), 805–835.

[216] Interviewee 5.

[217] Sirois; Hathaway, interview.

[218] Luoma, interview.

[219] Interviewee 5.

[220] Luoma, interview.

221 Interviewee 15.

222 Interviewee 5.

223 Luoma, interview.

224 Interviewee 7, July 7, 2010; Hathaway, statement, June 29, 2005.

225 Interviewee 15.

226 Sirois.

227 Hathaway, interview.

228 Interviewee 19.

229 L.H. Pelled, K.M. Eisenhardt, and K.R. Xin, "Exploring the Black Box: An Analysis of Work Group Diversity, Conflict, and Performance," *Administrative Science Quarterly* 44 (1999), 1–28; see also DeWitt C. Dearborn and Herbert A. Simon, "Selective Perception: A Note on the Department Identification of Executives," *Sociometry* 21 (1958), 140–144; Charlan Jeanne Nemeth, "Minority Dissent as a Stimulant to Group Performance," in *Group Process and Productivity*, ed. Stephen Worchel, Wendy Wood, and Jeffry Simpson (Newbury Park, CA: Sage Publications, 1992), 95–111; Allen C. Amason, "Distinguishing the Effects of Functional and Dysfunctional Conflict on Strategic Decisionmaking: Resolving a Paradox for Top Management Teams," *Academy of Management Journal* 39 (1996), 123–48.

230 Interviewee 5.

231 Interviewee 7, July 9, 2010.

232 Hathaway, interview.

233 Ibid.

234 Ibid.

235 Interviewee 5.

236 Sirois.

237 Interview with Michael Root, DEA Agent assigned to JIATF–South, July 8, 2010.

238 Interviewee 7, July 7–8, 2010.

239 Luoma, interview.

240 Sirois.

241 Hathaway, interview; interviewee 7, July 9, 2010.

242 Interviewee 7, July 8, 2010.

243 Luoma, interview.

244 Ockman.

245 Ibid.

246 Hathaway, interview.

247 Brooks; Sirois.

248 Interviewee 7, July 7–8, 2010.

249 Brooks; Sirois.

250 Interviewee 19.

251 Interviewee 9.

252 Interviewee 12.

253 Sirois.

254 Glenn M. Parker, *Cross-Functional Teams: Working with Allies, Enemies, and Other Strangers*

(San Francisco: Jossey-Bass, 2003), 10.

[255] Hathaway, interview.

[256] Sirois.

[257] Root.

[258] Interviewee 12.

[259] Ibid.

[260] Luoma, interview.

[261] C.W. Langfred, "Too Much of a Good Thing? Negative Effects of High Trust and Individual Autonomy in Self–managing Teams," *Academy of Management Journal 47* (2004), 385–399.

[262] Luoma, interview.

[263] Interviewee 10.

[264] Sirois.

[265] Root.

[266] Interviewee 5.

[267] Interviewee 10.

[268] Interviewee 13.

[269] Interviewee 7, July 9, 2010.

[270] Interviewee 13.

[271] Interviewee 12.

[272] Ibid.

[273] Interviewee 15.

[274] Ibid.

[275] Interviewee 13.

[276] Interviewee 15.

[277] Luoma, interview.

[278] Interviewee 13.

[279] Root.

[280] Ibid.

[281] Ibid.

[282] Interviewee 5.

[283] Interviewee 12.

[284] Booth.

[285] Hathaway, interview.

[286] Ibid.

[287] Interviewee 2.

[288] Interviewee 7, July 7, 2010.

[289] Root.

[290] Luoma, addendum, 2.

[291] National Research Council, *Maritime Security Partnerships* (Washington, DC: National Academy of Sciences, 2008), 85.

[292] Interviewee 5; Hathaway, interview.

[293] Luoma, interview.

[294] Interviewee 7, July 9, 2010.

[295] Interviewee 10.

[296] Luoma, interview.

[297] Interviewee 12; interviewee 10.

[298] Interviewee 12.

[299] Ibid.

[300] Interviewee 7, July 9, 2010.

[301] Root.

[302] Sirois, 3.

[303] Ibid.; interviewee 10.

[304] Interviewee 7, July 7, 2010; Luoma, interview; interviewee 5; interviewee 10.

[305] Interviewee 7, July 7–8, 2010.

[306] Ockman.

[307] A. Pirola-Merlo, C. Hartel, L. Mann, and G. Hirst, "How Leaders Influence the Impact of Affective Events on Team Climate and Performance in R&D Teams," *Leadership Quarterly* 13 (October 2002), 561–581; A. Pirola-Merlo and L. Mann, "The Relationship between Individual Creativity and Team Creativity: Aggregating across People and Time," *Journal of Organizational Behavior* 25 (2004), 235–257.

[308] J.A. LePine, "Team Adaptation and Postchange Performance: Effects of Team Composition in Terms of Members' Cognitive Ability and Personality," *Journal of Applied Psychology* 88 (2003), 27–39.

[309] S.T. Bell, "Deep-Level Composition Variables as Predictors of Team Performance: A Meta-Analysis," *Journal of Applied Psychology* 92 (2007), 595–615.

[310] Interviewee 12.

[311] Interviewee 7, July 8, 2010.

[312] Interviewee 12.

[313] Interviewee 15.

[314] Interviewee 5.

[315] Interviewee 13.

[316] Interviewee 12; Ockman.

[317] Interviewee 15.

[318] Root.

[319] Steve Sass, "Energy Security: A Global Challenge," U.S. European Command After Action Report, National Defense University, January 12–13, 2010.

[320] Interviewee 7, July 8, 2010; Sirois, 3.

[321] Hathaway, interview; interviewee 19.

[322] Interviewee 13; Sirois, 2.

[323] Interviewee 12.

[324] Interviewee 9.

[325] Sirois, 2.

326 Ibid.

327 Interviewee 5; Ockman; Hathaway, interview.

328 Luoma, interview.

329 Sirois; Ockman; Luoma.

330 Interviewee 12.

331 Interviewee 7, July 9, 2010.

332 Interviewee 5.

333 Angel-Schultz.

334 Ockman.

335 Interviewee 10.

336 Interviewee 13.

337 Jacquelyn S. DeMatteo, Lillian T. Eby, and Eric Sundstrom, "Team-Based Rewards: Current Empirical Evidence and Directions for Future Research," *Research in Organizational Behavior* 20 (Greenwich, CT: JAI Press, 1998), 141–183.

338 Grassley, 9.

339 JIATF supplements the rent paid by some of the foreign liaison officers whose housing allowances are insufficient even for on-base housing. Angel-Schultz, interview.

340 Ibid.

341 Sirois; Luoma, interview.

342 Hathaway, interview.

343 Ibid.

344 Sirois.

345 Luoma, interview.

346 Interviewee 5.

347 Interviewee 9.

348 Interviewee 5.

349 Luoma, interview.

350 Interviewee 10.

351 Interviewee 5.

352 Ibid.

353 Sirois, 2.

354 Interviewee 12.

355 Sirois, 2.

356 Interviewee 15.

357 Ibid.

358 Ockman.

359 Mathieu et al., 2008, 449.

360 A. Srivastava, K.M. Bartol, and E.A. Locke, "Empowering Leadership in Management Teams: Effects on Knowledge Sharing, Efficacy, and Performance," *Academy of Management Journal* 49 (2006), 1239–1251; J.R. Hackman and R. Wageman, "A Theory of Team Coaching," *Academy of Management Review* 30 (2005), 269–287.

[361] Mathieu et al., 2008, 450–451; N. Bennett, J.A. Harvey, C. Wise, and A. Woods, *Desk Study Review of Distributed Leadership* (Nottingham, UK: National College for School Leadership, 2003).

[362] Angel-Schultz.

[363] Interviewee 15.

[364] Hathaway, interview.

[365] Sirois; Ockman.

[366] Luoma, interview.

[367] Interviewee 15.

[368] Sirois.

[369] Ockman.

[370] Sirois.

[371] Hathaway, interview.

[372] Ibid.

[373] A former JIATF–South director.

[374] Interviewee 13.

[375] Luoma, interview.

[376] Ibid.

[377] Ockman.

[378] Sirois.

[379] Hathaway, interview.

[380] Luoma, interview.

[381] Angel-Schultz; interviewee 5.

[382] Ockman.

[383] Luoma, interview.

[384] Luoma, addendum, 2.

[385] Parker, 65.

[386] GAO, *Drug Control: Agencies Need to Plan for Likely Declines in Drug Interdiction Assets, and Develop Better Performance Measures for Transit Zone Operations*, November 2005, 17.

[387] Based on charts provided by interviewee 7, August 2, 2010.

[388] JIATF–South 2003 command brief PowerPoint presentation, courtesy of Sirois.

[389] Interviewee 19.

[390] Interviewee 7, charts.

[391] Luoma, email communication with authors, November 15, 2010, about draft final JIATF–South monograph.

[392] Placido; Sirois.

[393] Luoma, interview.

[394] Interviewee 7, July 7, 2010; Hathaway, interview.

[395] Interviewee 7, July 7, 2010.

[396] Interviewee 5.

[397] Riveles, 11.

[398] Luoma, interview.

[399] Hathaway, statement, June 29, 2005.

[400] Ibid.

[401] Interviewee 7, July 7, 2010.

[402] Interviewee 16; interviewee 7, July 7, 2010.

[403] Hathaway, statement, June 29, 2005.

[404] Placido; Sirois.

[405] Interviewee 13; interviewee 7, July 8, 2010.

[406] Luoma, interview; Hathaway, interview.

[407] Interviewee 19.

[408] Ibid.; interviewee 7, July 7, 2010.

[409] Interviewee 7, July 7, 2010; "Drug Submarine Found in Colombia," BBC News, September 7, 2008, available at <http://news.bbc.co.uk/2/hi/americas/915059.stm>.

[410] "Coast Guard Hunts Drug-running Semi-subs," CNN, March 20, 2008, available at <http://edition.cnn.com/2008/CRIME/03/20/drug.subs/>.

[411] David Adams, "Drug Smugglers Turn to Semisubmersible Vessels," *St. Petersburg Times*, April 11, 2008, available at <http://www.tampabay.com/news/world/article451245.ece>.

[412] U.S. Drug Enforcement Administration, "DEA Intel Aids in Seizure of Fully-Operational Narco Submarine in Ecuador," July 3, 2010, available at <http://www.justice.gov/dea/pubs/pressrel/pr070310.html>.

[413] Kevin G. Hall, "At $2 Million Each, Subs Become the Drug Transport of Choice," *McClatchy Newspapers*, 1, July 8, 2008, available at <http://www.mcclatchydc.com/2008/07/18/44739/at-2-million-each-subs-become.html>.

[414] Hathaway, interview.

[415] Stephen Meiners, "Central America: An Emerging Role in the Drug Trade," *Stratfor*, March 26, 2009, available at <http://www.stratfor.com/weekly/20090326_central_america_emerging_role_drug_trade?ip_auth_redirect=1>.

[416] Sirois, 2; interviewee 16.

[417] Hollis; Hathaway, interview.

[418] Executive Office of the President, Subcommittee on National Security and Foreign Affairs Oversight and Government Reform Committee, testimony of R. Gil Kerlikowske, Director, National Drug Control Policy, *Transnational Drug Enterprises (Part II): U.S. Government Perspectives on the Threat to Global Security and U.S. National Security*, March 3, 2010, available at <http://www.white-housedrugpolicy.gov/news/testimony10/3032010_nsfa_committee.pdf>.

[419] Hollis; interviewee 19; Luoma, interview; see also United Nations Office on Drugs and Crime, "Cocaine Trafficking in Western Africa," October 2007, available at <http://www.unodc.org/documents/data-and-analysis/Cocaine-trafficking-Africa-en.pdf>.

[420] Luoma, interview.

[421] Placido; Sirois.

[422] General David P. Fridovich, director, SOCOM Center for Special Operations, before the House Armed Services Subcommittee on Terrorism, Unconventional Threats, and Capabilities, March 11, 2009, 4, Internet resource.

[423] James Carafano, "A Better Way to Fight Terrorism," Heritage Foundation, May 18, 2005, available at <http://www.foxnews.com/story/0,2933,156732,00.html>.

[424] Gabriel Marcella, ed., *Affairs of State: The Interagency and National Security* (Carlisle, PA: Strategic Studies Institute, U.S. Army War College, 2008), 429, Internet resource.

[425] Comment from an under secretary of defense to one of the authors.

[426] James Carafano, "A Better Way to Fight Terrorism."

[427] Senator Henry M. Jackson, ed., *The National Security Council: Jackson Subcommittee Papers on Policy-Making at the Presidential Level* (New York: Praeger, 1965), 39. See in particular, U.S. Senate Committee on Government Operations, *Organizing for National Security: Inquiry of the Subcommittee on National Policy Machinery*, Sen. Henry M. Jackson, Chairman, 1961, 17.

[428] U.S. Pacific Command, Joint Interagency Task Force West, available at <http://www.pacom.mil/web/site_pages/staff%20directory/jiatfwest/jiatfwest.shtml>.

[429] Interviewee 15; interviewee 19; Hollis.

[430] Interview with a JIATF–West source who prefers to remain anonymous.

[431] A good overview and explanation of JIATF–South can be found in GAO, *Defense Management: U.S. Southern Command Demonstrates Interagency Collaboration, but Its Haiti Disaster Response Revealed Challenges Conducting a Large Military Operation*, 2, July 8, 2010, available at <http://gao.gov/products/GAO-10-801>. See also John T. Fishel, "The Interagency Arena at the Operational Level: The Cases Now Known as Stability Operations," no publishing data, available at <se2.isn.ch/serviceengine/Files/ESDP/95507/ichaptersection.../10.pdf>. For other examinations of JIATF–South, see also Lawner et al.; Darren Hanson, "Unity of Command: An Answer to the Maritime Homeland Security Interagency Quagmire," Naval War College, October 31, 2008, available at http://www.dtic.mil/cgi-bin/GetTRDoc?Location=U2&doc=GetTRDoc.pdf&AD=ADA494312>; Martin Lidy and Scott Feil, "Best Practices for Geographic Combatant Command Transformations: SOUTHCOM and AFRICOM," Institute for Defense Analyses, April 9, 2008, PowerPoint; and Curt Klun, "War on Drugs: Lessons Learned from 35 Years of Fighting Asymmetric Threats," Project on National Security Reform Case Study, 85; "National Drug Control Strategy 2010," 85, available at <http://www.whitehousedrugpolicy.gov/publications/policy/ndcs10/ndcs2010.pdf>.

[432] Department of Homeland Security, "Bottom-up Review Report," July 2010, 16, available at <http://www.dhs.gov/xlibrary/assets/bur_bottom_up_review.pdf>. See also Rick Nelson and Adam Isles, "The First DHS Bottom-up Review," Center for Strategic and International Studies, August 31, 2010, available at <http://csis.org/publication/first-dhs-bottom-review-1>.

[433] GAO, *Defense Management: U.S. Southern Command Demonstrates Interagency Collaboration*, 2.

[434] Interviewee 15.

[435] Sirois.

[436] Luoma, email.

[437] Luoma, interview.

[438] Christopher J. Lamb and Evan Munsing, "Secret Weapon: High Value Target Teams as an Organizational Innovation" (Washington, DC: National Defense University Press, 2011).

[439] There are several good descriptive pieces of work that explain aspects of JIATF–South's

performance over time. For JTF–4, see Miskill; Ahart and Stiles. For JIATF–East, see two GAO products: *Drug Control: U.S. Interdiction Efforts in the Caribbean Decline, and Drug Control: Update on U.S. Interdiction Efforts in the Caribbean and Eastern Pacific*. For JIATF–South, see Yeatman, 14–15. Dr. Stan Riveles has produced the best analytic evaluation of JIATF–South's current performance that we found, but it is in draft and for official use only: "Can Inter-Agency Organizations Succeed? A Review of the JIATF–South Experience," FOUO, Institute for Defense Analyses, undated. Other good sources of insights on JIATF–South—particularly the GAO report—are identified in note 417.

[440] Ockman.

[441] See, for example, GAO, *Defense Management: U.S. Southern Command Demonstrates Interagency Collaboration*, 9.

[442] This issue was raised by Richard Booth, who rightly noted that it would be helpful if Congress rewarded agencies for the level of cooperation that they extend to a priority national mission rather than merely focusing on a single quantitative metric.

[443] "Skelton, Davis Introduce Groundbreaking Interagency Reform Legislation," *Small Wars Journal* blog, October 2, 2010, available at <http://smallwarsjournal.com/blog/2010/10/skelton-davis-introduce-ground/>.

About the Authors

Dr. Christopher J. Lamb is a Distinguished Research Fellow in the Center for Strategic Research, Institute for National Strategic Studies (INSS), at the National Defense University. He conducts research on national security strategy, policy, and organizational reform, and on defense strategy, requirements, plans, and programs. In 2008, Dr. Lamb was assigned to lead the Project for National Security Reform study of the national security system, which led to the 2008 report, *Forging a New Shield*. Prior to joining INSS in 2004, Dr. Lamb served as the Deputy Assistant Secretary of Defense for Resources and Plans where he had oversight of war plans, requirements, acquisition, and resource allocation matters for the Under Secretary of Defense (Policy). Previously, he served as Deputy Director for Military Development on the State Department's Interagency Task Force for Military Stabilization in the Balkans; Director of Policy Planning in the Office of the Assistant Secretary of Defense for Special Operations and Low-Intensity Conflict; and from 1985 to 1992 a Foreign Service Officer in Haiti and Ivory Coast. He received his doctorate in International Relations from Georgetown University in 1986. Dr. Lamb has received the Chairman of the Joint Chiefs of Staff Joint Distinguished Civilian Service Award, the Presidential Rank Award for Meritorious Senior Executive Service, the Superior Honor award from the Department of State, and Meritorious Civilian Service awards from the Department of Defense.

Mr. Evan Munsing is a Subject Matter Expert at the Center for Strategic Research in the Institute for National Strategic Studies at the National Defense University. Mr. Munsing is a graduate of Bard College at Simon's Rock and the London School of Economics and Political Science. He worked at the Center for Strategic Research from 2009 to 2010, where he conducted research on national security organizational performance. He is currently attending Marine Corps Officer Candidate School.